# Truth Transforms Education

# Truth Transforms Education

## A FRAMEWORK FOR NEW SCHOOL LEADERS

**Antoinette Pearson, EdD**

ISBN-13: 9780998271804
ISBN-10: 0998271802
Library of Congress Control Number: 2016957595
Common Sense Learning, CANTON, MICHIGAN

# Acknowledgements

First, I want to thank all my many friends, my family, and my colleagues for supporting me in writing this book. Your words of encouragement truly helped me along this journey.

Special thanks to...

My friend Mrs. Thomas, who has always been the voice of reason.

My editor, Dana Johnson, for helping me to transform a manuscript into a book. I don't know how I could have finished without your expertise.

Principal Baruti Kafale, for special words endorsing this book. You are an inspiration for aspiring authors and education professionals.

My parents, Anthony and Bernadine Hoston, my very first teachers. You demonstrated how caring for your students (your children) means giving your all to ensure your students' (your children's) success.

My children and first students, Alexis, Casey, and Breann, who have helped me understand that true teaching is more than just saying what is right but modeling it as well.

My husband, Rodney, who has been my thought partner, biggest fan, and loudest cheerleader.

Finally, thank you to all the many students, families, and teachers I have had the pleasure of serving. I am humbled that I was chosen to serve you as a teacher and administrator. The impact you have had on me personally and professionally is immeasurable.

# Contents

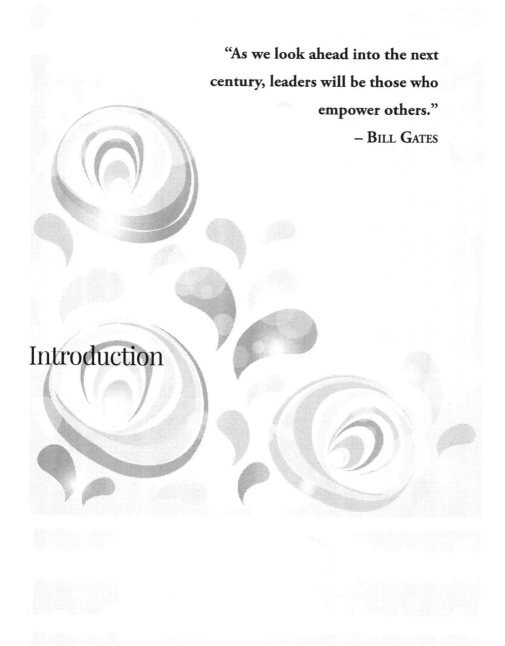

"As we look ahead into the next
century, leaders will be those who
empower others."
– BILL GATES

Introduction

# Introduction

I can't even begin to explain how excited I was to be asked to become a principal that summer. At that time, I had been dreaming about being a principal for a few years. As an assistant principal in one of the city's premier high schools, I knew what was needed to create a culture of academic success and felt I was ready to take on the challenge.

When the call came, I couldn't wait to find out to which school I would be assigned. It had already been narrowed down to two schools in a large urban community, one a K–8 building and the other a 5–8 building, both on the east side. Initially I was assigned to the K–8 building. Eager to get started, I visited my school a few days after the call. It was in a quaint neighborhood and appeared to be well kept. I found my way into the building and began to look around. It was adorable. There were small, colorful desks in classrooms and student work posted on boards throughout the halls. The building was one level and just the right size for me as the new principal. As I continued walking through the halls, watching custodians prepare the building for the new year, I grew more excited. I even had a wonderful conversation with the building engineer about the students and parents of the school. I couldn't wait to get started.

After exiting the building, I received a call with the unexpected news that the school that I had just happily envisioned myself leading as principal was going to be closed. I was informed of the decision to have my assignment switched to a school not too far from my original assignment. I was immediately flustered because as a first-year principal I knew I would have plenty to do to get prepared.

A few days later, I made a trip to my new assignment to see the school, hoping there would be no more stressful changes. The building was not totally unfamiliar to me. When I first started my educational career, I began at this very same school as a substitute teacher. I only vaguely remembered the specific details of the building's interior, but what I did remember was it had been very neat and clean. The principal then had been no slouch in keeping up the building. Now, my heart was broken—the appearance of my new school was the opposite of the first school I had visited days before.

Instead of pulling up to a mowed lawn, I noted that the grass around this school was overgrown. It looked as if the school had been abandoned or closed. The school did not reflect the surrounding neighborhood, which was lined with neat, well-kept homes. These homes were occupied primarily by retirees, who kept neatly manicured lawns with colorful flower beds. The tidy houses made the school look all the more unkempt.

Walking up the path to the front door, I reassured myself that the inside had to look better. After all it was just grass, and maybe this school was next in the landscaping schedule. Boy, was I wrong.

The wide, spacious halls were dimly lit. Paint was peeling from the lockers and walls. Walking farther into the school, I observed that the lavatories were painted black to keep the graffiti from being seen, but the dark paint left them looking dismal and dingy. Positive affirmation banners hanging in the halls were dirty and tagged with gang signs and additional graffiti. Every classroom seemed to have mismatched furniture and tattered books. The cafetorium, which served as both cafeteria and auditorium, displayed residual substances of past food fights on the walls and the ceiling. The main office was a disaster. Flyers and papers were plastered on the glass wall facing the hall. Student records had been left on the secretary's desk behind the counter. There were large amounts of paper—and stuff—everywhere.

Walking back to my car, I felt deflated and defeated. I sat in my car and actually began to cry. I wondered to myself what I had done to be punished like this. Here I was a new principal, with no secretary, no staff, no mentor, and no idea where I was going to round up the help needed to make this place look inviting for students. Understand I had been assigned to a school selected for restructuring because of being awarded a federally funded School Improvement Grant, with the Turnaround reformation model calling for replacement of the principal and fifty percent of the staff. Essentially, I was alone with no one to help me tackle this enormous task.

I had two choices. I could call and let my district know I didn't feel prepared to handle this assignment and decline the offer, potentially risking future opportunities for principalships. Or I could stick with the assignment, do my best, and hope it would work out. Not only did I opt for the second choice, I took it a step further. I decided I was not just going to do my best, I was going to pour everything I knew and all the resources I had into creating a great place of learning for the students and staff I didn't know, nor had I yet met.

And so began that long, arduous, and utterly frustrating journey. With the support of the one assistant superintendent the district assigned to help me with hiring staff, I was introduced to my wonderful first and only administrative assistant, who helped me weather the storm. With my limited network and her extensive knowledge of district procedures and connections with key facilities people, we started the physical transformation of the school. Still, I knew I also had to put some management systems and procedures in place to create a safe setting for staff and students. That burden was one I had to bear by myself. I alone knew how I wanted the school to look and how I wanted it to run. I knew the systems had to be stern yet flexible enough to adjust to the school population.

At the beginning of the school year, just a short three weeks later, students were amazed at how clean and bright the building was, scrubbed fresh and light bulbs replaced, among many other tasks completed. Several students were heard commenting about how different it looked and felt. However, the physical changes didn't change how students interacted with teachers and one other. Nor did the welcoming environment increase student compliance with school rules. Let's just say a five-minute passing period took more like fifteen minutes. We had a long road ahead of us.

By second semester, one month after Winter Break, the culture had shifted. Kids went to class on time; the multiple daily fights dropped to maybe one every two weeks; constant hollering by teachers was only rarely heard—it was a whole new environment. The culture of dysfunction and chaos was now one of purpose and respect. By the beginning of the following school year, the school had been removed from the state's persistently low-achieving list. What an accomplishment!

It would perhaps take a long time to tell here about all the many happenings in my first year as a principal, but through that experience, and definitely in the next five years I served as principal, I endured plenty of battles that left serious emotional scars and challenged my sense of purpose. I often wonder if I had had someone who was readily available to provide some practical insight, some real talk about this role, would I have had to endure so many of those battles? If I had been able to pick up the phone and ask the opinion of a colleague or mentor about a situation before making a difficult decision, how much easier would my life have been? I would often tell fellow principals that I would never want anyone to experience what I did with my first principal assignment. At that time, the difficulties were truly more than I thought I could bear. I would also share with colleagues that if I could provide a strategy or two to someone starting off in a new principalship, I would gladly and wholeheartedly offer my support.

It is with this mindset that the idea for this book was birthed. From my challenges, I have gained valuable insight into how new leaders can approach the principal role, the relationships, and priorities for their school. I want to share my thoughts with you, the new leader, to make your job a little easier. We all know this work is difficult, and each context is different. But if sound guidance were extended to us as we travel this leadership path, we would readily take it.

It is my humble and sincere pleasure to shape my experiences into such guidance, creating seven foundational principles I believe will help you stay grounded while doing this important work. By unearthing the truth about who you are and your purpose as a building leader, it is my desire that this truth will begin to transform your life and the lives of those you lead and serve. Good leaders transform schools. Great leaders transform not only schools but also lives.

Indeed, *truth transforms education.*

"The first responsibility of a leader is to define reality. The last is to say thank you. In between, the leader is a servant."

– Max De Pree

# Truth Provides Understanding and Transforms Educational Leaders

## Truth Provides Understanding

As a building leader, I have many times faced the difficult task of making a school decision without having all the information required. Or in some cases, the information I was given was not accurate. It is frustrating to be held accountable for situations—particularly less than ideal situations—where the decisions that led us there were made based on incomplete information.

Consequently, I have always emphasized, in my actions and words, being truthful and transparent to the people I work with. The state of emergency for many of our schools demands a sense of urgency from those leading them, pushing those leaders to create equitable places of learning that support teachers and students professionally, culturally, socially, and academically. To move forward, an unrelenting commitment is required to identify what is true and accurate about the status of the school. The effort to disrupt and concurrently improve upon traditional educational structures first requires defining that "truth."

One dictionary defines the word *truth* as "a verified or indisputable fact, proposition, principle, or the like; an obvious or accepted fact; actuality or actual existence."[1] Truth, then, is not arbitrary. The truth should not depend on how a person or organization plans to apply it to a situation. Nor should the truth depend on that person's or organization's agenda.

Along with truth, understanding is needed to provide the enlightenment and the power to apply these truths to make sound decisions. In other words, understanding goes hand in hand with truth. Understanding is defined by the same dictionary as "knowledge of or familiarity with a particular thing; skill in dealing with or handling something."[2] Understanding requires not only seeking facts regarding a situation but also thinking critically about those facts to fully grasp the situation. The quest for understanding is based simply on what is and not on personal biases.

In reality, truth and understanding are not black and white or simple concepts. Often, truth can be distorted, masked, or altogether lost within one's personal desires and ambitions. Additionally, truth can be hidden within one's fears or assumptions about a situation, a person, or an organization. The absence of truth is manifested in a variety of scenarios, but whatever the reason, the lack of truth always creates problems. Without complete, factual content, it is nearly impossible to have full understanding of a situation that encompasses several viewpoints. This incomplete picture hinders the making of sound and informed decisions and the initiation of appropriate actions. The lack of truth diminishes judgment and creates additional struggles, not solutions.[3]

To complicate matters further, there is also the "perception of truth" grounded in the moral compass of every individual. This perception of truth becomes the reality of individuals, shaping our thoughts, actions, and the world. This sometimes-misconstrued perception of truth can contribute to an incomplete or faulty process of decision making and solution development as well.

So, is truth a moving target? Will truth always be influenced by the special interests of a person or a group? Or can truth be collected using a rational approach and the instruments of an open mind and a listening ear?

Unfortunately, in education, the group with the loudest voice, the greatest number, the deepest pockets, or the most political influence has often shaped the truth.[4] These groups, many with minimal to no formal education training, have created the truth about how educational systems and structures, personnel, and instruction should look and feel. This perception of truth has smothered thousands of educators and administrators along with their ideas, their creativity, and most important, their educational practices. It has hurt millions of children. It has confused parents. It has created a multibillion-dollar industry that includes assessments, curriculums, textbooks, consultants, programs, and more.

Yet, for all these tools for success, the disparity of achievement has continued to widen between White people and people of color, the number of children living in poverty has surpassed the number of children in the middle class, misdiagnosing of children for special education services has skyrocketed, and discipline infractions for minorities students have accelerated phenomenally within the past ten years.[5] Admittedly, there has been a slight simultaneous increase in graduation rates as well as in students applying and going to college[6]; however, the same imbalances are seen in these improvements. Disparities in how students are served by education today are the result of decisions made based on the perception of truth held by political and financial leaders. This skewed truth has become the new normal.

How can education be transformed to reflect accessibility for all students? How can the inequitable distribution of resources, such as professional training, personnel, finances, technology, and other supports, be redirected to meet the needs of schoolchildren, their parents, and the community?

We must redefine the popular definition of "truth." We must allow unbiased decisions to drive honest and objective change that will begin to redevelop our educational structures and institutions.

Truth must transform education.

## Truth Transforms Educational Leaders

There is no question that our educational systems need a major overhaul. Many areas within all districts and schools should be restructured to meet the demands and challenges of our youth. These changes range from redefining school funding formulas to revamping curriculum, and from modifying teacher training to implementing instructional strategies to increase student engagement. The list is long. Yet, the most impactful change that will influence our youth begins in our schools. Change starts with those "boots on the ground"—building and classroom leaders who are interacting daily with our children.

I believe the leaders in the schools and classrooms are the one most important factor in the journey to transform the current educational systems. Yes, we school leaders have district mandates, national standards, and political pressures pressed upon us daily. And trying to manage the myriad of requests slows actions that support creativity in the development of school programs, systems, and culture. But leaders must feel empowered to lead in accordance with their training and expertise, and influenced by the relationships they have cultivated with the students and the communities they serve. Any inability to properly educate is not likely due to the lack of desire, talent, or skill but to the many disjointed variables placed upon school leaders and teachers by the public.

For building leaders, it has become difficult to navigate through the barrage of public demands and societal issues that challenge our students and families, especially regarding teaching and learning. Less than twenty years ago, you could walk into a school, see students sitting in neat rows copying spelling words from the board while the teacher was at his or her desk taking attendance. The teacher would present every bit of content to the students. Then, not many questions were asked about the validity of the content, and it was unheard of to challenge the thinking of the teacher about how content was delivered or when during the school year it was presented. The teacher was the expert and was to be respected as such by both students and parents.

Today, with the phenomenal increase in the advancement and accessibility of technology, not only can students access incredible amounts of information almost instantly, they commonly learn from a variety of these sources. Granted, there are some mistruths on the Internet, but no one would disagree that the desire for information and the speed at which we can attain it has altered our lives in ways we could not have imagined twenty years ago. This lifestyle change should be reflected in our schools as well. Today, it is almost impossible to run a school without engaging students with technology.

Additionally, this 'instant gratification' society has altered how people are engaged. No one wants to wait for anything. You can pre-order your coffee or meal from a restaurant, pay for it with your phone, and go into the store to pick it up without waiting. It is convenient, and it provides opportunities to spend time on all the other things we must do. So, if this is how many of our daily lives are structured, why do we insist on having students sit quietly in rows, with little or no engagement with peers or technology? Why do we expect them to sit and listen to a teacher for a fifty-five-minute class period while we ourselves struggle waiting ten minutes in a drive-thru line? These societal changes have affected how students develop socially, how they learn and interact, and how they engage. The fact is the bulk of content that we teach isn't changing, but how we empower students to think differently—more independently, collaboratively, and analytically—is the new challenge.[7] Our students desire more interactive and technologically infused learning, along with creative lessons facilitated by informed teachers.

This shift challenges teachers to restructure the traditional teaching practices learned through teacher education programs into more modern practices. Higher education programs are now understanding that their methods need to shift to meet the growing demand of school districts to employ teachers equipped to meet the needs of their students. However, teacher preparation is usually limited to instructional practices and subject content and lacks in student interaction and relationship building. Teacher training does little to prepare novice teachers for the social challenges they face with their students, particularly those teaching in urban areas with a historical context of poverty and academic failure.

What teacher training through higher education has not provided is being delivered through other means. For example, there are nonprofit organizations that have extended teacher education by providing intensive weeks of training and real-time coaching. There, additional attempts are made to develop contextual understanding for teachers regarding relationship building and cultural competency. Yet, although most of our teachers are adjusting successfully, they are greatly affected still by two pressing concerns: 1) the inequitable assessing of school progress to determine the success of a school, and 2) the struggle of allowing students to be discoverers of their own learning, with the educators removing themselves from the role of "sage on the stage" to become facilitators.

Ultimately, school leaders own the challenge of successfully educating students and training teachers, professionally and personally. These daunting tasks require a skilled leader, one who will take the risks needed to transform and disrupt traditional education through developing people.

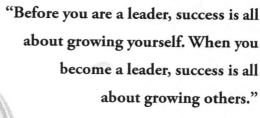

"Before you are a leader, success is all about growing yourself. When you become a leader, success is all about growing others."

– Jack Welch

Creating Great Schools

# Assessment and School Leadership: What story is being told?

We all have ideas of what a great school looks like. In our ideal "great school," teachers are caring and enthusiastic. Students are respectful and engaging. Classrooms are vibrant and have walls that talk, telling the story of learning. Everyone is safe, and students can participate in plenty of enriching courses, such as art, physical education, music, dance, and technology. Most important, all the students in the school are doing well, academically and socially, and can demonstrate their proficiency on any standardized assessments administered. Students are on grade level with their learning, and teachers are effective in their teaching. The few teachers and students who do not conform to the culture of achievement and respect established in the school are immediately weeded out.

This picture of the ideal school originated with and is driven by several factions: parents, business leaders, politicians, and community members. Unfortunately, these same ideals have created a dangerous cycle of reward and punishment based on ratings for academic progress in schools. Academic progress as measured by assessments is now a major component of educational reform that now seems to be driving reform initiatives, as in the federal Race to the Top program. The "bad schools" are restructured by replacing principal leaders or with shuffling teachers around. They are given scripted curriculum and are tightly monitored for a specific length of time, with ultimate closure looming if progress is not quick and sustainable. Resources allocated to the schools are limited and earmarked for special programming, such as literacy and math support, giving little flexibility of spending to the school leaders to meet the needs of their students. The subsequent rewards and punishments a school receives are based on the results of the local or national assessment instrument.

It is no wonder several stories of testing scandals have been reported in the media, of district officials, school leaders, and teachers involved in widespread cheating. The pressure is immense, and the stakes are high. Careers can be tarnished with poor evaluation ratings. A sole source of income can be lost. Meanwhile, the good schools are rewarded with accolades and financial incentives. Naturally, these schools attract and retain good leaders and teachers with little effort. For them, the cycle of success will continue because they will receive what they need financially and instructionally, reaping the benefits of being a good school. For the bad schools, it will be just the opposite—hard to attract good leaders and teachers, and hard to retain those who already work there.

Some educational policy makers and government entities have recognized that this cycle exists and needs to be interrupted. Hence, efforts are underway to attract strong leaders and teachers to low-performing schools using financial incentives. Some districts have even provided special authority and autonomy to leaders of these schools to help provide the means for creatively changing the culture of failure that has existed. Legislation and special federal funding (e.g. School Improvement

Grants) have helped to address these needs as well. But essentially, the only factor used to determine the success of our schools is the assessments given to our students.

In most U.S. schools, students will engage in two types of assessments: formative and summative. Formative assessments, such as quizzes or written summaries, gauge student learning through ongoing feedback that teachers use to modify their teaching strategies. Students use the feedback also to improve their own learning. Generally, formative assessments target the strengths and highlight the weaknesses of students, and they help teachers identify and immediately address areas of struggle.[1]

Summative assessments are used to evaluate student learning of identified concepts and standards at the end of a unit or a course. Information from these assessments is used mostly to determine success of schools, teachers, and instructional practices.[2] Indeed, assessments are important for districts and their leaders to identify what adjustments to make and where to place additional resources to support learning.

Although both formative and summative assessments are necessary and critical for informing teaching and learning throughout the school year, excessive testing has become the status quo for our schools. It is not unheard of for a school to administer assessments, such as end-of-course exams or academic progress tests to students every six to ten weeks. This does not include the state standardized tests required. In any given year, a school can spend six to eight weeks proctoring a minimum of three assessments. The extensive amount of time spent assessing can lead to test fatigue and shutdown. How will students be excited about learning when they feel they are testing all the time? And with instruction time cut significantly, when will this learning take place?

In addition to these potential time constraints, the appropriateness of using the results of assessments to determine school effectiveness remains a question. Results of assessments don't tell the whole story. They provide only a snapshot in time. Although trends in assessment results provide insight into academic progress in schools, the results themselves don't tell how that progress occurred or convey the challenges faced by the leaders, teachers, and parents. Results don't talk about the strategies needed and implemented to create a culture conducive for success. Results don't focus on how the leader rallied the staff around the importance of their work and its impact despite the constant negativity displayed about schools in the media or by legislators.

In these situations, the leader must be cognizant of how assessments and their results, good or bad, can alter the culture of their building with the staff and the students. This leader must be in tune with how to continue motivating everyone towards a goal that seems out of reach for those in a low-performing environment. In high-performing environments, the task is the same but may not pose the same seemingly insurmountable challenges. Still, motivating staff to strive beyond the district standards already met and to teach creatively and innovatively is the primary challenge for all.

The ability to spur on teachers to remain focused and motivated requires a strong leader. Additionally, this leader must be able to address the teachers having difficulties with shifting their thinking on how to teach their students. These leaders must be able to navigate the balance between encouraging teachers and challenging teachers to plan and instruct progressively.

Good leadership is required to transform education by creating foundational reform within schools. The success of these efforts hinges on strong building and classroom leaders. More specifically, capable building leaders are crucial to the process because they will create the culture of continued learning and professional growth needed for their staff.[3]

Further, research on the link between student achievement and the building of constructive climates and positive relationships shows a strong correlation to leadership. When leaders foster leadership in others, encourage people to solve problems, and build a trusting environment, student performance increases. Leaders must be willing to create a climate in which there is collegiality, open communication, collaboration, and conversation.[4]

Think about jobs you have had where the stress you faced daily wasn't because of the actual tasks you were responsible for but was a result of poor communication or a feeling of isolation. You do not desire to work in an environment that does not value you as a vital contributor. You do not want to fight to be heard or to have your ideas considered. Furthermore, you want to be under the direction of a leader who is inclusive and does not show favoritism. Most would agree that the peace of mind found in a good work environment is more important than having a couple of extra dollars in your paycheck.

## Types of Leadership: Which do you identify with?

As tomorrow's leaders of schools are being selected, many decision makers have firm opinions on the types of leadership they feel are needed to right the ship. In leadership training courses, educators have been exposed to several types of leadership styles, their benefits, and their risks. Some of the most common leadership styles are transactional, transformational, and servant leadership. Of the three, servant leadership is the most recent to emerge in the educational arena.

In transactional leadership, the model centers on the idea of a "give and take" relationship between the employee and the employer. The prime motivator in this something-for-something relationship is money. Most educators go into the field with the notion of helping children or their community, fully realizing that becoming wealthy is not the driving force. But in the current state of our system, making money seems to be more of a factor than in times past. Teachers are being offered incentives for having large amounts of students rank proficient on standardized tests, and incentives are being offered for working in impoverished communities, to highlight a few examples.

Whereas transactional leadership may seem to be all about business, transformational leadership is about connection. Transformational leadership focuses on the leader sharing a sense of purpose together with the staff. Transformational leaders are considered charismatic motivators with the ability to develop strong interpersonal relationships. These relationships allow staff to participate in the management of the school in matters such as decision making and delegation of responsibilities. With transformational leadership the leader is in the forefront, directing and motivating staff to produce. The leader's role is to fire up individuals to perform for the leader and for the overall success of the organization. However, displaying the constant charisma needed to maintain interpersonal relationships with those being led can become taxing over time. When the energy of the leader begins to wane, the enthusiasm and the drive of the staff in moving forward toward organizational goals reflects the decline also.

In contrast to transformational leaders, servant leaders are not driven by any self-interests. The servant leader steps back, desiring to support the interests of the followers above those of the organization and self. Guidance, empowerment, and creation of a culture of trust are the foundational blocks of servant leadership. Critics of servant leadership declare that the leader loses sight of the organizational goals as they are empowering the followers because there is minimal direct instruction for those who might need it. However, a strong servant leader provides an organizational framework and structure while still empowering. The overall goal of any organization should be refined and executed as a collaboration between the leaders and the followers. This act of engaging others is empowerment. Followers who feel vested from the inception of the journey with this leader will work towards the goals with little additional motivation from the leader. Why? Because it is an "ours" goal and not a "yours" (the leader's) goal.

It would be safe to say that many school leaders have the capacity to become proficient in managing the school climate. Managing requires establishing rules, procedures, and systems to create order. This managing is a series of top-down decisions made solely in support of the leader's design. Some daily areas, such as leading team meetings or coordinating school activities, are delegated to staff members based on what the leader views as their strengths. Yet, there are some hiccups that come along with being a leader who manages in isolation. Those leaders who develop policies and procedures without input from staff run the risk of losing momentum when putting them into practice. If a policy is ineffective, perhaps because of inconsistent implementation or gaps in the policy itself, others see the failure as a result of the leader's idea alone. Whatever caused the failed policy, there is no tone of ownership from the staff because, well, they did not help create it. They were never asked. They were simply told what to do.

Servant leadership holds the belief that organizational goals will be achieved long-term only by first facilitating the growth, development, and general well-being of the individuals who comprise the organization. The desire to serve people overrides organizational objectives.[5]

Staff works together to ensure that students' needs are being met because they have been supported with their own professional growth. They feel completely vested in the success of the organization because they have contributed to the building of policies, practices, and procedures. They have been encouraged to take risks and to be creative. They have a support system that challenges them and allows them to continually improve. The idea of community is the reality.

"You've got to be willing to lose
everything to gain yourself."

— IYANLA VANZANT

# Servant Leadership and Your Assignment

## Characteristics of Servant Leadership

During my first years as a teacher, I worked under a principal who was stern about rules and policies. Strict adherence was not only for the students but for the staff as well. In my opinion, this principal didn't value us as teachers, as she invoked a spirit of fear among the staff. Teachers and staff followed the rules out of anxiety about retaliation and retribution. Some of my colleagues remained extremely stressed with the thought of the principal even stepping into our hallway.

I felt this was a terrible way to maintain order and to run a school. I have always believed a leader should respect teachers for the college graduates and professionals they are. Through this experience, I concluded that a leader who consistently micromanages has issues with trust and control. Although it was early in my teaching career, I vowed that if I became a school leader one day, never to interact with people as this principal did.

At the time, I didn't know that how I wanted to engage others as a leader was a form of servant leadership. It wasn't until my graduate courses and dissertation studies that I began to learn about leadership styles, particularly servant leadership. This exceptional level of commitment to service, although universal and timeless, was first named and described by Robert K. Greenleaf in the 1970 essay "The Servant as Leader":

The servant-leader is servant first... It begins with the natural feeling that one wants to serve, to serve first. Then conscious choice brings one to aspire to lead.... The leader-first and the servant-first are two extreme types.... The difference manifests itself in the care taken by the servant-first to make sure that other people's highest priority needs are being served. The best test, and difficult to administer, is: Do those served grow as persons? Do they, while being served, become healthier, wiser, freer, more autonomous, more likely themselves to become servants?[1]

In reflecting and expounding upon Greenleaf's concepts of servant leadership, thought leader Larry Spears named ten critical characteristics of the servant-leader.[2] These are **listening, empathy, healing, awareness, persuasion, conceptualization, foresight, stewardship, commitment to the growth of people,** and **community building.** That is not to say that no other qualities exist that exemplify the notion of a leader putting the individuals in the organization first, and himself or herself second. These characteristics, however, are most commonly associated with servant leadership. A summary of each of Spears's characteristics is described briefly in the following chart.

## 10 Characteristics of Servant Leadership

| | |
|---|---|
| **Listening** | Listening allows a leader to tune in to what others feel and believe. Listening provides understanding, which helps facilitate meaningful and productive conversations. |
| **Empathy** | Empathy allows a leader to be cognizant of the diverse backgrounds of parents, staff, and students. Empathy helps a leader to avoid hasty judgments about people and their situations. |
| **Healing** | It is difficult for a leader to care for others when facing personal challenges. Emotional state impacts decisions and actions. Healing must start with the leader; only then can a leader help to make others more whole. |
| **Awareness** | Awareness keeps a leader on alert, open to his or her surroundings, and observant of the school climate. A leader is in the "know" with everything happening in the building. A leader must also be self-aware. |
| **Persuasion** | Persuasive dialogue about changing the status quo should include validating data as well as supporting arguments that bring understanding. Buy-in, essential for progress, is hindered by force or intimidation. |
| **Conceptualization** | Conceptualization calls for a leader to envision a broad and layered picture into the future rather than to focus on the short-term and the everyday. Conceptualization also allows a leader to examine problems broadly. |
| **Community Building** | To build community, a culture of trust and collaboration must exist. Once everyone feels that they significantly contribute to the organization and its success, there is increased momentum toward the organization's goals. |
| **Stewardship** | A leader is committed to serving the needs of the individuals of the community, but not in a controlling manner. |
| **Commitment to the Growth of People** | A committed leader nurtures both the personal and professional growth of all individuals. A leader values and acknowledges hard work and contributions, involves others in decision making, and listens to ideas and suggestions. |
| **Foresight** | Always reflective and understanding of lessons from the past and circumstances of the present, a leader uses that knowledge to determine steps for the future. |

Traditionally, leaders have been valued for their ability to communicate and make decisions. John Rosenblum, a business school dean, says, "Servant leadership at its heart is an openness, an ability to listen, and an ability to speak in a way that engages people directly affected by the choices to be made."[3] Rosenblum comments further on the value of **listening**: "I see this as a key leadership quality of the servant-leader style and advocates for leaders to ask themselves if they are really listening to their subordinates."[4] In addition to allowing leaders to gather information for decision making, intentional and genuine listening can make a world of difference in relationship building and in making the members of an organization feel heard and validated.

Listening must be coupled with **empathy**. As an educator who has served in the urban core, I was unable to personally relate to many circumstances my families faced. Yet, I intentionally sought understanding to support them. Empathy, loosely defined as the ability to understand and share someone else's emotions, is a fitting characteristic for one who practices servant leadership successfully. The meaningful relationships formed through empathy, leadership expert John C. Maxwell suggests, are based on the leader's genuine love for the people, and the followers' respect in kind and their willingness to follow.[5] I myself witnessed that the relationships developed through the intentional desire to support and care for my families created bonds of trust that helped the student become successful.

I realized early on that challenges and difficulties in my personal life impacted my interaction with others, including those in my professional life. I admit that when I was personally wounded I was not at my best with decision making or reacting to school incidents. **Healing** is one of the great strengths of servant leadership—the healing of self and of others. Healing starts with the individual and, as wholeness is found within, so the individual can influence others positively, helping to bring them into wholeness as well. To bring about such healing, servant-leaders must truly care about people and sincerely want them to grow as individuals.[6]

The ability to self-reflect and identify personal shortcomings as well as to recognize potential organizational conflicts is paramount as a servant-leader. **Awareness** of self and surroundings keeps leaders on alert. Greenleaf profoundly states that "able leaders are usually sharply awake and reasonably disturbed."[7] C. F. Abel emphasizes that "awareness requires an act of faith on the part of the leader. It is the belief that the leader has the strength and ability to face the problem and find the solution."[8] In servant leadership, there is no ignoring internal or external issues to avoid dealing with them. A constant sensing of school climate is critical as is tuning in to the physical environment. For example, there is nothing more dangerous than an out-of-control lunchroom with three hundred students and food. When on lunch duty, you must be aware of the abnormally loud noises that usually indicate conflict. Similarly, unusual quiet is often a red flag. But even amid sometimes seeming chaos, a self-aware leader always finds peace within.

Leadership experts and authors Barry Posner and Jim Kouzes note, "The most admired leaders are also leaders who make their followers feel valued, who raise their sense of self-worth and self-esteem."[9] Servant-leaders are deeply **committed to the growth** of every individual within their institution, recognizing the tremendous responsibility to do everything within their power to nurture the personal, professional, and spiritual growth of employees.[10] This commitment is the ultimate example of **stewardship**, where the needs of others are put first. "Achieving this level of service can only be obtained through a true commitment to people by genuine concern and love."[11]

A leader committed to growth and to serving others provides opportunities for meaningful conversation to occur around the staff's professional development and the students' social, emotional, and academic development. Through dialogue, a servant-leader can persuade staff to adjust as needed to further goals for developing both people and organization. My experience with moving staff to change always depended on substantiating points with solid evidence. The rationale provided information for teachers to fully understand, be open to persuasion, and make informed choices to adjust willingly, not by coercion or intimidation. "The servant-leader relies on **persuasion** and is effective at building consensus within groups."[12]

Finally, as a servant-leader, you ultimately strive to **build a community** of trust where support, respect, and true collaboration exist. Staff may meet your efforts to create a community with some resistance because their view of the school is expectedly more limited and focused. As the leader, you are looking at the bigger picture, analyzing the many moving pieces that impact the school and the students. The ability to look at a problem from a **conceptualizing** perspective means that you must think beyond the routine realities. For many managers, conceptualization is a characteristic that requires discipline and practice. As a servant-leader, you are called to seek a delicate balance between conceptual thinking and daily focused approach.[13] A servant-leader also depends on **foresight** in determining direction for an organization and its people. Foresight considers past experiences and current realities, using them to make decisions, plan, and forecast likely consequences for the future. The quality of foresight is more an instinct than anything. "The ability to foresee the likely outcome of a situation is hard to define but easy to identify."[14]

Again, although this list of servant leadership characteristics is not exhaustive (a few more have been added in recent years of research), these described qualities do serve to communicate the power that servant leadership offers. It can be a fearful decision for a leader to make priorities of empowerment and staff development before meeting the organizational goals. To some, that decision hinges on being a rebel. How dare you seek to empower and develop people? That's not why you were hired. You were hired to bring up test scores, to make the school safe, to encourage parents to be an active part of their student's school career. And what does people development have to do with those concerns? Absolutely everything!

Who does the daily work in the classroom? The teachers do. As much as building leaders would like to think we have total power and control of what happens in a building, we would be snatched into a very different reality if all the teachers were to walk out at the same time. So, developing the most important resource in the school is crucial for true transformation and sustainability to occur. Furthermore, the results of the time spent in building capacity of teachers will be reflected and felt long after the current leader moves to another school. In fact, the culture of trust and collaboration will be embedded such that the new leader will have no other choice but to maintain this positive element of the school culture, even if there are some instructional practices that need to be addressed.

It is important to note that choosing to practice servant leadership does not indicate any form of low self-concept or self-image. On the contrary, it requires a leader to have an "accurate understanding of his or her self image, moral conviction, and emotional stability to make such a choice."[15] Only a leader confident in and comfortable with his or her own strengths and shortcomings can acknowledge the talents of the staff and use those talents to catapult the school toward success. Accepting the existence of shortcomings will indeed be a servant-leader's strength in the long run.

As leadership roles are shifting and being redefined, leaders are becoming more like facilitators, catalysts, or creators of social change. These leaders must know themselves and must know and understand the population they serve and be willing to meet its needs at all costs. This means you, as leader, may have to stand on priorities that aren't necessarily the priorities of the powers that be. This means you may have to justify your priority-driven decisions to meet certain standards. As a servant-leader, you will find that your way of prioritizing and addressing some situations does not represent a widely accepted viewpoint. Your distinct perspectives and consequent actions may be frowned upon and questioned repeatedly. But, strategically, it is imperative that staff development and empowerment are simultaneously addressed along with organizational goals.

You may fear that this juggling act may cause one area to suffer because of the impossibility of devoting equal time to both. And truly, in measuring efforts in terms of time, empowering staff and addressing organizational goals will not be equitable. In fact, more time should be dedicated to empowerment. We all acknowledge that an organization must work towards multiple goals at the same time; however, focusing on staff empowerment consequently impacts organizational goals. "An organization founded on these principles [of servant leadership] has the potential to generate the greatest reward for the organization as whole."[16]

## So Where Do You Begin?

The day has arrived when that coveted leadership position you researched, applied to, and interviewed for has been entrusted to you. You have gone to school for several years to complete your masters and doctorate degrees. You have participated in many professional development seminars, read hundreds of pieces of educational literature, and have worked in the trenches with your colleagues for years. You know the mental and physical demands. You understand the challenges of working with children and their families. All these experiences and demonstrations of leadership spelled out in the application and discussed during the interview process have impressed upon the interviewers that you are up for the challenge and ready to begin.

With the appointment, the congratulations and elation soon wane, and reality comes rushing in. You knew you would probably not get one of the "better" schools because the principals in those buildings stay until they retire or are appointed to a central office position. But you were praying you would not get one of the lowest performing schools. I mean, you are new and recognize you have some learning still to do. You find that your building was recently identified for improvement measures based on the past years' assessment data. And although it was stated by those who hired you that support will be available in the form of a weekly visit by a leadership coach, you cannot help but think that those visits will have little effect in the face of the day-to-day grind.

With so much at stake as the new leader, anxiety can set in and cause frantic thoughts to surface. You are aware of the tremendous task ahead of you and know many people are counting on you to make success a reality sooner than later. Under the pressure of expectations and being a leadership novice, you would appreciate some direction on how to chip away at this mountain. You know that you are going to need a lot more support than an occasional stop-in by a leadership coach.

Each situation is different for each leader, but there are principles all school leaders should be cognizant of as they move into their new position. Framed through the lens of servant leadership, these principles provide leverage in approaching this new leadership challenge and arm you with insights for feeling prepared and capable.

These Seven Principles are 1) know who you are, 2) know who you serve, 3) know how to gain acceptance, 4) know how to manage rejection, 5) know how to practice humility, 6) know when to leave, and 7) know your impact. In the following chapters, we will explore each principle and understand how each can guide you through every leadership position from beginning to end.

> "We cannot change what
> we are not aware of, and
> once we are aware, we cannot
> help but change."
> -SHERYL SANDBERG

# Know Who You Are

## Servant Leadership Characteristic: Awareness

I don't think I'm going to make it. I feel sick. As she tries to suppress the thoughts in her head and the sick feeling in her stomach with a gulp of strong black coffee, she focuses on how she wants the day to go. This is my first day with all my staff. What will they think of me as I present my PowerPoint to them? Will they immediately sense how terrified I am? Did I make the right decision in accepting this job?

The staff begins to enter the library. The new staff, wide-eyed and nervous, quietly walk to seats in the front. The veteran staff enter joking and laughing about some of last year's episodes, wondering if certain kids are coming back. As she shuffles her stacks of papers for the tenth time and surveys the library tables steadily filling with staff, she quietly says to herself, "It's all about the kids." As she repeats this phrase, she reflects on how she ended up at this point in her career.

She thinks about her middle-class childhood where her parents had steady jobs and made sure everyone ate dinner together daily. She recalls her involved lifestyle, spearheaded by her parents, and how the activities she participated in were based on her family's faith. She remembers how her parents constantly emphasized the importance of siblings sticking together and that everyone has a purpose in life. Her parents made it a point to impress upon her the value of a college education and of helping others. She often heard her father say the ultimate sacrifice is helping others become better so they can help themselves.

*These thoughts slowly calm her down. She knows she made the right decision. Her desire to become a building leader is to help others become better. Yes, I am here for the kids. I am here for my teachers. I am here to provide support. I absolutely made the right decision.*

*"Good morning, everyone! And welcome back to the beginning of this school year,"* she says with confidence. *Her sense of purpose is renewed.*

It takes a lot for you to stand in front of an audience and attempt to transform and redirect their ideas to one goal or set of organizational values. First, you must get past your thoughts about how you think the staff may be judging you based on your appearance and demeanor. Then, you must get past the misconceptions you may hold based on your first impressions of the school. *They didn't seem concerned about presentation or looking presentable to the public.* You've heard some good things about the staff, but it seems that more of the negative was the focus of the conversation. I mean, the district did make some changes because the leadership before you did not work out. But do remember that everyone deserves a clean slate. Historical context is fine as a reference, but it should not be used to draw premature conclusions about the school or the staff.

You have inherited a vision from the previous leadership. You have read it, and it seems to have some good points. Still, you feel it could use a couple of key phrases like "equity and accessibility" or "creativity and innovation." But why do you want those phrases added to your vision?

Will adding them give the perception that these ideals will exist in your school? Do you believe in what these words represent? Furthermore, is the vision a reflection of what the staff will be working towards? And can you lead them if you don't know what you value?

This last question is important because, essentially, the organization reflects the values held by leadership.[1] No vision, mission, or plan of action can occur without 1) understanding the historical data and context of your school and, more important, 2) understanding your own values and how they drive your decisions and actions.

## Finding Your Starting Point

Today's society provides us with technological devices that allow us to be inundated with instant feedback, continuous communication with others, and real-time information from around the globe. This technology often includes a Global Positioning System (GPS) that can give explicit directions from where you are to any destination you desire. A GPS can be a lifesaver, particularly for those of us who are directionally challenged. They save us from time lost looking for a location by following human-provided directions or deciphering paper maps. And though a GPS can sometimes give weird directions or take us on a scenic route, they are accurate, mostly. This navigation system, however, requires human input. You cannot get directions to the destination until you let the device know *exactly* where you are positioned. Such is the case with people.[2] That is, you must let your staff know exactly what your values are before you can begin the journey together.

How do you begin to create a common vision for the organization you are leading if you don't know what you value? As a leader, you must be confident in what your purpose and mission is—first, for your own life, and then, for the organization you are leading. Think of a couple that is making the decision to get married. Both have an idea of what their married life should be. One feels that postponing children is important so they can establish their careers. The other feels that they should have children early in their lives so they will have more time to enjoy them and the grandchildren that follow. This conversation may prevent some couples from getting married, but as in any relationship, it is important that both parties understand what their values are before proceeding.

Also, you must know why these values are important to you. In the marriage example, maybe the one who wants to postpone having children grew up in a family where the parents never had the chance to achieve their goals, putting everything on hold to start a family, perhaps earlier than expected. And maybe the partner was born to older parents who were not active in their own lives and not actively involved in their child's life. As their child grew older and more active, the parents grew older and more inactive. Each person in the relationship, therefore, has a rationale for feeling strongly about when to have children. Their personal experiences frame the values they hold around being parents.

How do you begin this journey of reflection to name what is valuable to you? We all have an idea of what we feel strongly about—perhaps democracy, free will, honesty . . . you know that list. But why do you value honesty? Because valuing honesty is the right thing to do? But why is valuing honesty the right thing to do? Who said that we should value honesty and why?

These are just some of the types of questions you need to ask yourself around the terms you use to describe yourself and your leadership style. It is one thing to name a characteristic, but to understand why you are naming it and how this value was forged in your life is an essential exercise in gaining awareness. As you begin to identify those values within yourself that have helped create the individual and leader you are, use the following exercise to help crystallize and reinforce them.

## Principle 1: Know Who You Are
### ❖ A Practical Exercise ❖

Using a journal or notebook, complete the steps below to tap into and reflect on your core values and beliefs. Doing the exercise over multiple sessions may be helpful in allowing time and various situations to bring thoughts and ideas to mind.

1.  List ten personal characteristics that you feel make you a good leader.

2. Write one or two sentences about why you chose each of the ten characteristics.

3. Rank the ten characteristics from most important to least important in leadership.

4. Choose the top five characteristics.

5. Are there specific events in your life that you can connect to the top five characteristics listed? Write about those events as best as you can remember.

These connections, these stories with the most vivid and genuine descriptions, these memories you can still physically and emotionally experience when recalling the story through writing—these are the foundations of your moral compass.

These characteristics have resonated throughout your life, helping you to make choices through their deeply emotional and mental associations. These are the characteristics that helped shape who you are. Through this exercise, you will get a sense of your priorities and your purpose in deciding to become an educational leader. This clearly defined purpose helps to bring perspective on what is meaningful and valuable to you as you set systems and procedures in place. These values should help forge and develop a specific "feel" for the culture of the organization you lead.[3]

As I reflect on my life's experiences, I can begin to understand how I am grounded in certain values. This moral compass has supported all my leadership decisions and allowed me to prioritize tasks accordingly.

Although the journey has not been easy, understanding what is important to me and why it is important to me has granted me an internal peace.

These are the values and principles that influence my approach to life, my relationships with others, and my actions:

1. I always seek to be in alignment with my faith. I know that my greater purpose is to serve.
2. I prioritize. My family emphasized a clear order for life: faith, family, others, and then me.
3. I strive to help others. With whatever influence I have, I seek to use that influence to better the lives of those around me.
4. I protect and advocate for those who do not have the means to do it for themselves.
5. I use the good and the bad to grow personally and to teach others what I learned from those experiences.
6. I set goals but remain flexible. Despite how clear a plan I develop, I should always be ready to change it up when setbacks occur.

It is important to recognize the key values and principles that govern your thinking and behavior. Understanding why you do what you do helps you to become and stay grounded. This strong foundation provides a place for you to stand on and not be swayed towards things that do not align with your values. Take the time to shine the light on your values before you begin this journey in leadership. Remember who you are and why you chose this path rather than allowing others to define who you are.

## Thoughts on Knowing Yourself

- Leaders know who they are.
- Reflecting on life experiences and exploring the values that have been prominent or consistent in your life is key to understanding who you are.
- Reflect on how your values impact your interactions with people. Do you need to adjust your behavior to align with these values?
- Reflect on how your values impact your ability to make decisions. Do your decisions reflect your values?
- Be willing to recognize and acknowledge your biases. Be mindful of them when you make decisions to ensure equity and fairness.
- Being confident in who you are allows you to withstand any challenge that confronts you.

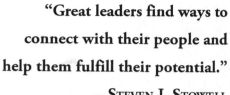

"Great leaders find ways to
connect with their people and
help them fulfill their potential."
— Steven J. Stowell

Know Who You Serve

## Servant Leadership Characteristics: Listening, Empathy, Stewardship

S am is a small-framed sixth grader. He has a reputation of being defiant and is considered an "X factor." Sam can go into any classroom, and within ten minutes, set the whole place off, initiating complete havoc in the room. The outcome of Sam's antics is always the same—being put out of class and, depending on the severity of the disruption, given a pending suspension. Some days when Sam enters the building, it appears that he is going to have a calm day. He greets me and quickly scurries to class, catching up with some of his friends along the way. He is occasionally seen in the halls during passing time, but his behavior is nothing beyond the typical middle-school boy. But most days when he enters the building and doesn't speak or make eye contact, he is going to have one of those days.

One morning when Sam doesn't speak to me, I take the time to simply ask what is wrong. I had never thought of asking him before. Sam looks down at his shoes and stands in his tracks as if stuck in cement. After a few moments of silence, he states that he just wants to go back home. Not sure if he is sick, we call his mother. Upon her arrival, she looks at Sam and shakes her head. Going out the office door, she is fussing at him, letting him know that he will stay in school and that he cannot come home all the time.

Over the next few weeks, the same incident occurs every two or three days. I continue to tell Sam that he will stay at school. One day, he shares with me, with tears in his eyes, that he needs to get home to his mom. It *turns out, she is being physically abused and Sam considers himself to be her protector. Sam had been acting out so he could stay home and save his mother.*

Car shopping, house hunting, choosing a restaurant, navigating relationships…big and little decisions implore us to do our research. We spend countless hours on the computer comparing prices, features, and usefulness of products on which we plan to spend perhaps thousands of dollars. We read articles and reviews about the product. We ask friends if they have had any experiences with the product or service. We google reviews of restaurants we want to try to see if there are positive comments on the quality of the service and food. If multiple reviews are even slightly negative, we are quick to eliminate them from our choices so we can narrow our options further. We invest time and energy with researching because, honestly, we want to get the most for what we spend. It is disappointing to spend money on a product that does not meet our needs or expectations. It leaves us upset and not trusting of that company or their product.

When it comes to relationships, we all have our standards for the type of person we feel will be the best companion for us. These standards include physical traits, familial background, career aspirations, and educational foundation, just to name a few. When we find someone who passes that first screening, we invest time in learning beyond what is seen on the surface. Digging deeper begins with many hours of conversation by phone and online, as we probe for more substantive answers about who this person is and what he or she offers. Communication through technology sometimes evolves into in-person communication. When we agree to be seen in public with this person, the relationship is evolving. Not yet knowing if this is "the one," there is still plenty of time and energy being used to screen this individual. Becoming committed is a big step in anyone's life and should be handled with much care.

It is only natural to take your time to understand what responsibili-.ties you will assume with a purchase or with committing to an individual. Who has time or money to haphazardly misuse? When we hear of individuals who make impulsive, expensive purchases or who seriously commit to an individual within hours of getting to know one another, we are appalled that they would not be more thoughtful. We label them as reckless, irresponsible, and even foolish.

But are district, building, and classroom leaders doing this same type of extensive research on our children, their families, and their communities? It is often stated in public forums or written in district and school vision statements that students and their families are valued. So, why aren't schools doing more research to understand what priorities we should be setting for our students' learning? Why are schools doing only minimal research on the families and the communities they are serving? For some schools, the research that could seriously impact student learning and family involvement appears to be nonexistent. The fact remains that the actions that follow from this belief in the value of students and their families should be visible beyond the words in a vision statement.

## Our Schools

I think we would all agree that having support at home for the work being done at school, academically and socially, is crucial. In fact, many believe that family support is the key to improving academic outcomes of our students. In many schools, you will see local school community organizations, parent teacher associations, and other parent groups posting or distributing information about monthly meetings. Information may also be posted in offices, in hallways, on notes sent home, and on school websites, to keep parents informed and to announce opportunities for parents to volunteer. Some schools have parent–student–school compacts, or pledges, that outline the school's expectations for parents and students. This document also states parents' expectations for the school as it relates to student learning and the overall school culture.

Even with all these family engagement tools being developed, implemented, and utilized in our schools, the efforts barely scratch the surface of what is effective in engaging parents. The endeavors are sporadic at best. Although the intentions are good, many of these efforts are pre-structured with a specific goal in mind, with little room to deviate to address any real concerns that may be generated by participants during the actual development of the tools. Also, the end products are created without needed input from families expressing what they would like to see occur in their school.

Additionally, often the parent organization meetings have already been planned, in some cases, using a predesigned curriculum or a previous years' format. Are the needs of parents the same from year to year? Or does that mean we didn't meet parents' needs last year so we must address them again this year? The attempts to engage parents are honorable but are inconsistent in implementation and even with capturing the voice of the "real family." The voices of parents are rarely heard to address the real-time concerns they are facing. Sadly, some schools that are recipients of federal funds may implement many of these initiatives out of compliance. Although this may not be the case for all schools, many fall within this category. Consequently, with the goal of making efforts to reach parents only for compliance's sake, we tend to undervalue and underutilize the members of the communities we serve, both parents and their students.

Let's ponder this thought. Why is education one of the few fields in which we professionals attempt to develop solutions to problems without methodically analyzing the context of the situation first? Consider this thought as well. Noncertified individuals, such as business people and politicians, propose and implement solutions to address the current academic and social struggles of the schools, using only basic information about our schools.

Schools, leaders and teachers alike, plan a full school year of instruction, committing to using specific instructional strategies and practices aligned to a pre-packaged set of standards without gathering the necessary information about the students we will be teaching. Furthermore, districts and schools set stoic rules and policies for academic and behavioral standards with the expectation that school leaders and teachers will implement them with fidelity every fall. And although the aims of this preparation are good, we tend to miss the critical piece of information that will help us all be successful—the students. For example, districts implement strict attendance policy regarding the number of tardy or absent days a student can accumulate during a semester. Exceeding this designated number results in automatic failure of a course. Has consideration been given to how students are transported to school and from what distances? If a student successfully passes all assignments within the course but has exceeded the tardy limit, is it fair to give the student a failing grade?

We apply these rules generally to all situations and we have little to no understanding regarding the root causes for why particular actions by students and parents are taken. We expect learning to occur by any means necessary. It is understood that there is a need to have high expectations and clear systems and structures in place to create an environment conducive to learning, but the desire to create the environment often discriminates against those we have created the environment for. These actions of discrimination instead of acceptance are reflective in our inability to be flexible and contextual with each student and situation. We are less than adaptable regarding students' learning styles and familial conditions. We leave little room for error to occur, which yields adverse conditions in which our students must perform. Because of the blanket application of policy, the ongoing negative impact of our systems on our students gives them and their families a sense of failure and hopelessness. Consequently, the results are usually harmful to the students' overall psyche and demeanor towards educational institutions and their teachers.[1]

Generally, we educators do not acknowledge the need to revisit and overhaul our daily structures and practices although suspension rates continue to rise, dropout rates continue to increase, and student performance only slowly improves.[2] We will, however, adjust minimally, continuing to forge through with the same basic set of standards and values, with only a slight shift in perspective and conduct. In our minds, we have developed "an understanding" as to why our students are in this current academic state of failure. Our theories help to justify why things are as they are and why it has been necessary to put into action certain policies and practices. And even though we truly believe we are correct in our analyses and conclusions about the current educational situation, we have minimal evidence to substantiate our claims.

Essentially, our assumptions, or perceptions, have developed our theories. Naturally, assumptions are rooted in biases developed over many years. No one wants to acknowledge that we all have biases, let alone admit that these biases contribute to possible inequitable practices. But these perceptions, often misperceptions, have influenced how we behave and act, even in our professional lives. Pointing out this unconscious process is not an indictment against any one individual or group of individuals. Nor is it an accusation against the training and expertise of those in the schools charged with educating our youth. However, this mental processing of how our biases influence our actions, a practice carried out by all humans, requires us to be strategic in how we evaluate the context of each school, keeping first in mind the students and the community in which the school is located.

One tool that can be effective in helping educators to hold biases in check and decision-makers accountable is the "ladder of inference." The ladder of inference is a model originated by organizational psychologist Chris Argyris[3] and notably applied by organizational learning expert Peter Senge in his book *The Fifth Discipline: The Art & Practice of the Learning Organization*.[4] The ladder of inference describes the thinking process that we undergo—usually without realizing it—to move from a fact to a decision and subsequent action. The ladder sits in a pool of available data, or the reality and facts we are exposed to. The steps of the thinking process are the rungs on the ladder. At the top is the action taken. The complete steps of the thought process, moving from the bottom of the ladder to the top, are as follows:

- Experience pool of facts or observable data.

- Filter the facts based on beliefs and experience, choosing which to pay attention to.
- Interpret facts by adding cultural and personal meaning.
- Make assumptions based on the meaning added.
- Draw conclusions based on the interpreted facts and assumptions.
- Develop or update beliefs based on these conclusions.
- Behave and take "correct" action based on beliefs.[5]

Because our beliefs help determine how we filter facts from the entire pool of observable data, an unintended loop can be created. In continually selecting certain facts, we may incorrectly reinforce their interpretation and ignore reality altogether. The danger of our reasoning process is that we may jump to conclusions based on missed facts and skipped steps. Therefore, it is imperative that at each stage of the ladder, we ask ourselves what we are thinking and why. By applying the ladder of inference, you can train yourself to get back to the hard facts and use your beliefs and experiences constructively, rather than allowing them to limit your field of judgment.

Following this step-by-step reasoning can lead you to better decision-making and help you to avoid unnecessary mistakes and conflict.[6] There are other benefits as well. As a leader, understanding and using this thought process benefits everyone by increasing your awareness and self-awareness. It also allows you to be able to clearly explain to others your decisions and actions, thus increasing transparency and building trust. Last, when making inquiries into any situation, you are better able to ask more effective questions about others' actions.

Again, there is nothing wrong with having a general idea of how a functional, inclusive system should be structured and how operational and instructional practices should be implemented. However, we must avoid using blanketed solutions to diverse contexts and situations. These general solutions create a culture of mistrust, disrespect, rebellion, and they sometimes harm the spirits of the children we serve.[7] This culture of mistrust can be seen in many of our schools today as evidenced by the lack of families participating in such school activities as parent–teacher conferences, or by unacceptable statistics of student discipline infractions and student population trends of a school. This data supports that people do not want to be a part of a school if they do not feel respected or valued.

Solutions framed by assumptions occur in many of our schools today. However, building leaders can begin to change these practices by being intentional with seeking information about their students and parents. Both informal and formal methods of collecting data help provide the necessary information to gauge how schools are creating an inclusive environment for students and their families. These activities for gathering information can be spread strategically throughout the school calendar year.

Greeting parents in the hall each morning is just one opportunity to solicit feedback. The conversation does not have to be lengthy but should be meaningful and direct, such as "How do you think the school year is going so far for your family?" One formal opportunity to gather information is through surveys created through external providers or by the school. Additionally, schools can schedule chat sessions where students and families sit down in an informal, relaxed setting to answer questions and engage in discussions on various topics prompted by the school facilitator leading the meeting.

All these strategies provide viable information that not only can be used to meet students' needs but also help to create a culture of respect and trust. The gesture of taking the time to hear the voices of the students and parents is appreciated. Moreover, when invaluable information gathered from student and parent surveys or interviews are used to create programs and initiatives or to provide feedback on current systems, students and parents feel more included in the school community. Customize a plan for your school that incorporates the voices of many by completing the exercise that follows.

## Principle 2: Know Who You Serve
### ❖ A Practical Exercise ❖

Use a journal or planner to reflect on, plan, and execute the steps below to help you identify and address the needs of the people you serve.

1. Create an appropriate tool for collecting feedback from various groups of stakeholders.

2. Schedule time for students, parents, and teachers to offer their ideas about the development of goals for the school using the tool.

3. Use the information gathered to identify the top three priorities of each group of stakeholders. These priorities will drive initiatives to be implemented to support each group.

4. Create committees of stakeholders to serve during the planning, implementing, monitoring, and evaluation phases of new initiatives. You can ask one or two individuals from each stakeholder group to serve on committees, personally expressing your desire for them to fully participate in the process.

5. Allow committees to generate programs, with you serving as a facilitator for accountability and guidance.

6. Celebrate the successes no matter how small!

The gathering of information should not begin and end with students and their families. It is necessary that the school leaders and instructors that serve them engage in intensive reflection as well. We must facilitate deep dives into why we think and act in certain ways within our schools, and we need to do this frequently. These honest conversations will serve as a reminder to building leaders and staff that the work is ongoing and the school will always call for improvement. By having leaders and teachers share their own reservations, concerns, and biases, a culture of collaboration and trust is formed. Often in our schools, teachers feel isolated in the workplace, particularly those in the higher grades. Rarely are opportunities available for them to work with other teachers in planning or reviewing student work and data. Teachers are often closed off in their classrooms, carrying a burden they think is exclusive to them alone. By creating time and space for these reflective practices, communication about how to address the challenges within the school will help make creating and implementing solutions easier and more attainable. Currently established staff meetings or professional learning communities can be used for doing this important work.

Knowing and understanding the community we serve is key to creating equitable and accessible schools for all children, despite our human challenges with addressing social issues. Leaders and teachers should be provided with cultural proficiency (CP) training. This training should be ongoing and help staff in appreciating the power of relationships and respecting the diverse values of students in their classes. As the staff becomes more proficient through this training, the results will be reflected in the types of assignments given to students, the diverse curricular materials introduced, and the genuine respect shared between staff and students.

"Cultural proficiency is a mindset, a worldview, a way a person or an organization makes assumptions for effectively describing, responding to, and planning for issues that arise in diverse environments."[8] CP training brings three areas to mind that are crucial when transforming organizational structures: presumption of entitlement, oppressive systems, and lack of awareness of the need to adapt.[9]

Our current educational systems were designed by those who also designed our government system: White, Christian, financially stable men. As a result, the systems hold embedded barriers that support gender, racial, and socioeconomic inequities. Those who share the characteristics of the system's designers tend to fare well and have been taught to expect a certain level of respect, power, and privilege. This sense of entitlement and lack of awareness regarding the suppressive actions of the system have continued to compound adverse conditions for minority groups. We educators know that learning is maximized when students have all their needs met, including the need to feel safe. So how can students that are different from the founders perform in an environment where they are made to feel inferior, whether intentional or not?

Leaders can lessen the effects of such adverse conditions by requiring CP training for all school staff, whether they work closely with students in the classroom or hold the keys to the custodial closets. Training in CP "is proactive and provides tools that can be used in any setting, rather than activities and techniques that are applicable in only one environment; is values based and behavioral, not emotional; can be applied to both organization practices and individual behavior."[10]

Focusing on training leaders and teachers in cultural proficiency is well worth the effort as it will create sustainable change. Meaningful time spent learning about our students and community must become the priority. These efforts will begin to shift the pendulum towards increased student achievement, holistic child development, and family inclusion.

We must know who we serve before we can decide how to serve.

## Thoughts on Serving

- Leaders know who they serve.
- Reflect on why you chose the field of education. Try to be specific and concise about the moment or event that directed you to education.
- What are your professional beliefs around the purpose of education?
- Create that space for teachers to express their opinion and ideas that contribute to the culture of collaboration in the school.
- Empathy is understanding the student's situation and does not denote having low expectations for students.
- There is no such thing as "not enough time" when it comes to learning about the people you are leading and serving. Time invested in the beginning yields great rewards in the end.

> "Earn your leadership every day."
>
> – MICHAEL JORDAN

# Know How to Gain Acceptance

## Servant Leadership Characteristics: Foresight, Commitment to the Growth of People, Building Community, Conceptualization

He often wonders if he is indeed making a difference as principal. He has been in his position for over six months, and it has been a grind. Since he assumed leadership of a low-performing elementary–middle school, the central office has made many demands on him. The stakes are high, and he knows things have to turn around—and quick.

He finds himself doing a tightrope walk between pushing the teachers and motivating them. He knows that too much pressure in an already intense environment pushes some teachers over the edge, causing them to shut down or leave their position outright. He also senses an urgency in the teachers' need to feel and be motivated daily. This feeling is reflected in their planning, their instruction, and their interaction with students.

He feels that progress is being made but still has some doubt in his mind. That Sunday night, just as he is sitting down to send out his weekly notes to the staff, he sees an email message from the lead on one of his elementary teams.

"Mr. Stevenson,

The team and I just wanted to thank you for your encouraging words and actions that you give us daily. Although we know we have lots of work to do for our students, we all have agreed that we feel confident we can get it done because you believe in us and support us. We know you have a lot to do, but just know we have your back like you always have our backs!"

*As he begins to type the notes, he smiles to himself. That was just the little nudge he needed to keep focused on what he had been purposed to do.*

We all strive for acceptance—acceptance by family, friends, and even complete strangers. It is an awesome feeling when people agree with you, support you, and get behind a cause you are fighting for. Having a following can be a powerful thing. And this power can influence change within an organization, affecting people's thinking and behavior and actions. When we are accepted, we feel empowered. We feel that there is no limit to what we can accomplish. We work harder. We stand taller. We strive higher to achieve more and more and more. But getting others to accept you is sometimes hard to do. Just how do you get people to accept you for who you are and what you believe? And more, is it possible to be accepted by everybody?

## Striving for Acceptance

In any leadership position, it is important that the people you have been charged to lead know who you are and what your purpose is. They need to know the values and principles with which you govern yourself. These values and principles should be applied to generate a vision for the organization. They will also help create a plan of action with specific strategies that you feel are necessary to achieve the vision. The individuals you are serving need to know and hear you articulate this vision for the organization. Notice I said that they need to "hear" you. It is not a good practice to write words on paper and leave it to the individual to interpret what they mean. It is unlikely that others will follow a leader they consider cryptic. A better dynamic is created when the leader of the organization takes the time to clearly and verbally define the vision.

Not only will this articulation provide clarity and eliminate individual interpretations, it will also allow people to see how personal this vision is to you. The passion and depth with which the vision is communicated shows how committed you are to the vision. People want to work with and for a leader who truly believes the words of the vision they created. This passion will inspire and motivate others to join in the journey with you. In verbally communicating with people, your personal values will be revealed. People will see what makes you who you are and begin to understand why you behave the way you do.

One aspect of gaining acceptance is for people to understand why you were appointed or hired in to this leadership position. Receiving a title does not automatically elicit trust from people. Nor does having the appropriate credentials and relevant experience. For some, it's just the opposite. Your placement may signal that you are "one of them" and are there to push the district's agenda, regardless of what is best for the students. The people you lead must believe that you are working for the good of all students and that you will support them, as educators, in their craft. This can be accomplished only by sharing about yourself and your ideas for the organization. Of course, this conversation does not guarantee acceptance, but it begins to lay a foundation for trust.

Let's pause here for a moment and focus on communication. This word is always thrown around when groups of people are expected to work harmoniously with one another. It is said that work cannot be effectively accomplished by a team if those involved don't communicate with one another. I am in total agreement with this statement, but we need to add some depth to the purpose of communication beyond getting a job done. First, communication provides an opportunity for all parties to clearly understand what each other is thinking. Now, this opportunity occurs only if everyone is honest and transparent in their thoughts and feelings. Failure to do so is the single biggest issue with communication. In instances where work doesn't progress smoothly, barring unforeseen external circumstances, it is often because someone failed to be completely honest and transparent.

But why do we try to hide information? Do we feel that if we keep certain information from our team it will protect our image? Do we feel that if we hold back certain information it will protect others from unseen dangers? Do we feel that some of the information is irrelevant or too much for the team to comprehend?

Lack of honesty and transparency in communication is largely because of one reason—to avoid conflict. By withholding some information, I do not have to explain why something was done or not done. I do not have to worry about hurting someone emotionally. I do not have to worry about someone not understanding, forcing me to discuss further information in a manner that may be perceived as demeaning. I can avoid provoking emotional responses from others. But that is just the thing. We cannot avoid dealing with inevitable emotional responses because we are humans, and humans are emotional. However, a good leader takes this truth into account and intentionally crafts communication to both validate the emotional responses that will exist and provide all the facts needed to be honest and transparent. That is, a leader will not avoid communicating openly because of fear of how people will respond. A leader accepts the reality the truth creates and works to help all parties accept that reality in a dignified manner that supports and validates all.

Now let's go back to communicating the vision and how this creates an arena of trust. Not only is communicating the vision important, it is just as important how you communicate the vision. People tend to forget that how you use your voice and body is as important as the words you are saying. I know this may seem like Communications 101, but it begs to be discussed. If the way I am communicating is loud, harsh, and direct, with a steady cadence compounded by minimal eye contact with the listeners, the vision could be perceived as a directive. This gives the perception that there is no other option but what has been told, that there is no room for adjustment, and that questions need not be asked.

Yet, if the vision is communicated with eye contact, pauses, emphasis on certain words, with the voice gently rising and falling with changes in speed, listeners will perceive the thought and consideration being given to the words. It softens the atmosphere and allows people to feel comfortable seeking clarity. It also provides the opportunity for people to push back on some ideas and opens dialogue about refining plans for the vision. Think about it: Depending on how my mother called my name, I either thought I was in trouble or not. Tone and body language matter. Your delivery conveys the kind of leader you will be. From this first conversation of length, the staff will generate an assumption of how approachable, flexible, and committed you are to supporting them. This initial communication can create an opening for collaborative work to begin or it can lock down the already narrow route between leaders and their staff.

While you are initiating this channel of communication, you must admit your inadequacies to your listeners. *Inadequacies? You mean I should let the people I have been charged to lead know that I don't know everything? I should let them know that I have shortcomings?* Absolutely! A leader does not want to be perceived as knowing it all. This type of leader is thought to be a micromanager, resistant to suggestions, and uninterested in self-reflection or growth.

Admitting your inadequacies now does not create an excuse for underperformance or for skirting responsibilities and accountability later. It does mean that you acknowledge that you are willing to learn. This admission creates a forum for suggestions and ideas from staff, who will feel valued because they have an opportunity to fill the gap that exists within your foundational knowledge. What staff would not want to be able to help the organizational leader create a plan to address a need or challenge in which they have extensive knowledge? Again, the fact that you are sharing such delicate information creates a sense among the group that you are willing to be open to some scrutiny. It is more likely that people will admire your honesty and transparency than question your appointment.

Finally, it is imperative that you acknowledge the experience and expertise of the staff. Verbally express your appreciation for the work they have accomplished prior to your assignment, especially amid the challenges they faced daily. Take the time to identify the resulting highlights of the school. Be clear that you have taken the time to understand the history and context of the organization and that you are humbled to be able to work with a set of talented individuals who have worked diligently to bring the school to this current point. Thank them for their past work and for their decision to work with you as the new leader. This allows people to feel deservedly valued and open to accepting you. Imagine the resistance and ill feelings if the new leader was to immediately bash past efforts by focusing on all that needs improvement and never acknowledging what has gone right thus far.

But the "elephant in the room" must be addressed as well. Everyone knows, whether verbally stated or not, that there is a need for improvement. There are no perfect organizations, and your job is to lead the efforts that continue to make things better. Granted, some areas of improvement are more obvious than others, but identifying these areas should be immediate and strategic. You don't want to step into the leadership role and continue with the same unproductive actions that have yielded little or no results. Prioritization of these identified areas should occur next, keeping in mind that consideration be given for targeting areas that yield quick wins. What are those areas that can show positive results quickly and motivate the staff to continue working towards the school goals?

You must acknowledge that although the organization will continue doing what has been successful, adjustments will be made so that more successes can occur. You must state that the tasks will indeed be difficult and may appear enormous, but they won't be impossible if addressed collectively. This prepares everyone for upcoming changes, some drastic, and provides your staff with a sense that you understand the challenges and are willing to work with them, not over them.

This is so important. An attitude of "Do as I say and not as I do" is detrimental to building a culture of collaboration and trust. Nothing will leave a more indelible impression on the minds of the staff than seeing their leader working alongside them to meet goals. This means sitting in meetings, going through the data, and asking questions together. This means engaging in professional development activities with staff. This means working with students and their families, along with the teacher, to accomplish a task. Your actions are more powerful than any words you can ever say and provide credibility to your track record and proof of your work ethic.

As the arena of trust is developing, begin to lay out the plan for the organization's future. The plan presented should not be concrete or rigid but should serve only as an outline that is open for modification. Assure the staff that the plan is not yet complete and requires input from them. By presenting a rational framework, it allows them to understand that you have done extensive research on the issues facing the organization and have developed serious thoughts on the next steps. By providing a platform for input, you reassure the staff that you are placing trust in them, valuing their expertise, and inviting them to contribute to the design and implementation of the plan. Specific individuals may spearhead components of the plan as fitting their skill sets and interests.

One of the most challenging functions for any leader is to communicate often and remain sincere when doing so. When tasks are assigned, it is extremely important to allow people the time and space to make progress. They do not want someone breathing down their neck and looking over their shoulder every moment of the day once given a task. Yet it is just as crucial to create opportunities for them to share their progress, to receive honest feedback, and garner praise for what has been accomplished. Many leaders miss this mark, either intervening excessively or not showing up until near the end of the task, either providing too much feedback and praise or not enough. Finding the balance between being present and stepping away is key.

Insufficient feedback on assignments in progress makes staff feel like they are working in isolation with no purpose, no end goal in mind. Timely, honest feedback is needed for continued development and growth of the organization just as it is needed by students monitoring their learning. This feedback may be uncomfortable to give in some cases, particularly if the task is not on pace to meet a deadline or has some incomplete components. It is necessary to relay this information to the assignee, but it is also necessary to be mindful of the message emanating from your voice and body during the conversation. The tone and disposition of the leader can derail the momentum of staff members, causing them to be resentful and become resistant to collaboration and change. On the other hand, your tone and disposition can also encourage and motivate staff to work harder and smarter.

Above all, you must remain sincere and genuine. People know when you are faking. We all have a sixth sense for detecting when someone is talking rhetoric and fluff. It is imperative to always imagine yourself in the shoes of others and ask yourself how would you like to be treated in the same situation. This might be difficult, especially when the work being done may not be meeting the standards you have envisioned. Building capacity in people will require some thoughtful conversations and delicate prodding and directing for some. In any case, the staff must feel that your actions as the leader are an effort to build their skill sets as well as to move the organization forward. Increasing your own abilities to communicate, empower people, and build community will, like all skills, require practice. Use the outline below as a plan to respectfully lead an organization through change.

## Principle 3: Know How to Gain Acceptance
### ❖ A Practical Exercise ❖

When presenting any initiative, plan, or procedure, consider the following steps to begin communication, invite input, and refine the final product:

1.  How will you communicate the plan to staff? Consider the type of format (e.g. small-group forums such as professional learning communities, a general staff meeting, etc.). The format may depend on the size and timing of the task and the parties involved.

2.  Does the presentation acknowledge current success in areas similar to the area now being addressed?

3.  Be specific about why there is a need for adjustment to the current program. Use as much data as possible to substantiate this stance.

4.  How will you respond to criticism from staff regarding the proposed plan? Be sure to be calm and respectful when dissension is voiced.

5.  Allow time for feedback to the presented plan. Determine beforehand if feedback will be collected during the time of the presentation or afterwards. Be specific about how feedback will be used.

6. Be open to possible restructuring of the plan.

7. Simply have an honest, sincere conversation with staff. Approval is not impossible to achieve!

Over time, as you implement and polish this process, people will begin to accept and honor you for your integrity, your honesty, and your ethics. Being accepted should not lead you down a path of arrogance or self-righteousness. Instead, acceptance should be a reminder that people believe in the work and in your leadership. Positive results should lead to your feeling confident in taking on and accomplishing larger and more challenging goals in the future.

But realize that not everyone you lead will accept you wholeheartedly. There will always be a portion that is resistant to change. Still, the voices of those who are not on board should be heard. The reasons for their resistance are significant and need to be understood. For example, there could be a misunderstanding that critics feel can't be publicly discussed. The reluctance to approach you as the leader may have made it even more difficult for those staff members to operate in the organization. Taking the time to meet them on their terms and in their space opens a level of personal communication and confirms your commitment. You must be sure to listen and filter out the noise, seeking the nuggets of truth within. Ask questions such as, "Is there something I missed or neglected to address?" They may never be totally won over by you, but they will respect that you feel responsible for listening to and understanding everyone.

Some staff members who are not on board will make more than noise. Regardless of how many attempts are made to collaborate, engage, and seek understanding about their thoughts and ideas, there will be some who refuse to work with the group. They will seek to derail the progress. These individuals can be toxic to the overall culture of the organization. It is crucial to identify these individuals immediately so that intense intervention can occur. There are usually two possible outcomes with these individuals: 1) They will be uncomfortable being the only one not working toward the goals, so they will seek to leave, or 2) They will learn to operate in compliance only, never being vested completely, until they become ready to leave. Nevertheless, be prepared to have people such as this in your organization. It is inevitable. And remember, if there is no one resistant to the change, then maybe your vision and plan aren't changing much of anything at all.

What I have shared is not a failsafe recipe for attaining acceptance because each setting and situation is different. Yet there are some common themes that resonate universally. These words are designed to spark your thinking, generate productive conversation, and hopefully, transform actions.

## Thoughts on Acceptance

- Leaders know how to gain acceptance.
- Be strategic in including staff throughout the process of developing plans.
- Tap into staff talent when addressing areas of concern or growth in the organization. There are many who can provide strategies and solutions.
- Use the momentum from staff buy-in to accomplish more tasks.
- The work cannot be accomplished alone. It truly takes a collaborative effort.

"The ultimate measure of a man
is not where he stands
in moments of comfort and convenience,
but where he stands at times of
challenge and controversy."
– DR. MARTIN LUTHER KING, JR.

# Know How to Manage Rejection

## Servant Leadership Characteristic: Empathy, Listening, Awareness and Persuasion

T*he rollout of the new lesson plan template is not going very well. Just one month in and teachers are complaining a great deal in their professional learning communities to the team leads about how laborious their planning has become. Less than half the staff feels the template is helping them to be more thorough with their planning. And the majority of this same group are reluctant to spend time completing the tasks that proper use of the template calls for.*

*However, it is now imperative that a standardized lesson plan template be used throughout all grades. Based on assessment data and daily walk-throughs, the leadership team had observed some major gaps with time on specific instructional practices and strategies that supported student academic development. Although Principal Jones hadn't wanted to be as prescriptive as requiring a universal planning template, she knew that she and her team had to change the course, instructionally.*

*Principal Jones tries to bring better understanding of the template to those who personally request a meeting with her to discuss their concerns. Most of these meetings have ended up becoming venting sessions. They have left her feeling beat down, wondering if maybe this decision had not been the right one, as so many are complaining. She had always said that she would never forget what it was like to be a teacher. She understood the daily pressures of being a teacher in an urban school. And she tried desperately to*

*keep that in mind as she made decisions that would directly affect teachers'*
*work. But this planning was crucial to the success of the students, and she*
*knew it had to be concise and thorough.*

*In the teachers she has already met, Principal Jones has intentionally*
*searched for some validity to their angst and concern, something besides sim-*
*ply being against change. Taking some of these ideas back to her leadership*
*team, she decides to have teachers come together to modify the areas they feel*
*are most challenging. During this meeting, she has also presented to them the*
*rationale for the template, using data for support. It is her hope that revisit-*
*ing the template with the assistance of the teachers will help to alleviate the*
*pushback. She is not naïve to believe that everyone will buy in. However, all*
*voices will be heard, and her decisions will always be based on doing what's*
*best for the children.*

Just as acceptance elicits feeling of elation and motivation, rejection
can wreck your whole sense of self-worth and drive. A few naysayers are
tolerable; half is unthinkable. But when more than half of your people
are naysayers, it is demoralizing and sweeps you toward a feeling of defeat. You begin to question your abilities as a leader. You question your
decision to accept the position. You question your thought process on
how the very idea to be a school leader was generated. Within yourself
you are asking, "But how can *everyone* hate the idea?"

Keep in mind that the degree of fear of change is often proportional
to the level of rejection that occurs. Change signals to humans that we
are not doing something right and that we need to be fixed. We don't

want to be told we are broken although we understand change is necessary and inevitably will occur. For some people, it is how we introduce the change and the speed of that change that determines the reaction.

Change is constant, even when not initiated through decisions made by the leadership of an organization. Influences from the outside world require schools to adjust as well. For instance, technological advances have tremendously accelerated how information is gathered and disseminated, including in schools. These advances greatly impact how we teach students and the methods we use. In this example, it is obvious that the need to change along with the circumstances does not mean that anything wrong was being done in the first place. Change in organizations, then, should not be automatically viewed as negative and should be presented by leaders as an opportunity to meet the needs of an ever-evolving society. Leaders should deliver a clear message for why specific changes are necessary and deliver that message in a non-threatening and non-insulting way.

Proposing change is a delicate, potentially dangerous path for leaders to travel. Some followers will say that they do not know how to do anything else. Some believe there is no need for change if what they have been doing has been successful so far, especially as compared to neighboring schools or districts. Then there are those individuals who have been with the organization for many years. They have seen several leaders come and go. They have seen initiatives begin and fizzle. They feel no sense of urgency to change because, in their mind, this time and leader will pass, as like the others before. Various perspectives held by individuals in the organization may lead to the rejection of your ideas. Furthermore, the greater the number of people who think negatively of your plans, the more difficult it will be to change the course.

Especially in the face of rejection, leaders do not sulk and turn inward. To serve the community, leaders reach out to all those involved and provide yet another opportunity to collaborate. The following exercise provides a step-by-step process for moving rejection into acceptance, all the while building community and empowering people.

## Principle 4:  Know How to Manage Rejection
### ❖ A Practical Exercise ❖

Record in a journal, planner, or notebook the steps of this exercise as your organization revamps a rejected plan or procedure.

1.  Identify areas of concern about specific plans or procedures from staff through surveys, small-group meetings, staff meetings, or other appropriate gatherings.
2.  For each area of concern identified, assign teams to propose a solution with a rationale to substantiate all suggestions.

3. Staff teams present suggestions, which are voted upon by all staff in a predetermined setting.

4. Revise relevant plans to reflect accepted suggestions.

5. Present plans, highlighting clear goals, a timeline, and role expectations. Be sure to identify who will serve as support during the implementation of the plans.

## Growing from Rejection

Even with dutifully referring to and implementing the ideas in the previous chapter and this current chapter, rejection is still likely to be a reality for you in one form or another. What does rejection say about you as leader? Or does rejection say anything about you at all?

Overwhelming rejection can cause serious doubts and constant questioning about what you have done wrong. You may think of yourself as a failure or unfit to lead. However, rejection is an opportunity to grow—it is not a negative judgment of your character. Whenever there is growth, expect there will be some discomfort and pain. Think about a new tooth coming in. It is uncomfortable and bothersome. Sometimes the pain can be debilitating. Yet when the tooth finally breaks through, the discomfort subsides. Such it is when an idea is rejected. But do be mindful of the opportunities that come between rejection and acceptance. This is your chance to grow stronger and renew your commitment, not give in.

First, rejection induces self-reflection. Often, we find little time to think deeply about what we are doing or what we did until we have failed. We do not necessarily look inward to assess where we need to improve; it is much easier to point to external factors as cause for why our plan was not accepted. But true leadership growth and development hinges on asking ourselves the hard questions about our motives and intentions. What was the purpose for my action or behavior with this issue? What did I truly want to accomplish? Who was I considering when this idea was developed? When a leader begins to drill down to the root cause for taking a certain action, there should be some discomfort. Hopefully, there will also be some revelation that proves useful in moving forward.

Naturally, rejection creates a place for humility. It reminds you that even as a leader, one person cannot run an organization alone, no matter how intelligent or gifted. It's impossible! Everyone needs help. When you grapple with why your best ideas (according to your own thinking) are rejected, you need to pause to consider those who are working with you. Ask yourself, Did I include their voice, ideas, or opinions before I created this initiative? Was there a collaboration time created to meet with stakeholders to gather their opinions? Did the fear of not having control of the situation influence why others were not included?

Rejection can also increase the drive to be better and do better. Maybe the idea was rejected because it did not totally encompass all the necessary components to move things forward effectively. Maybe the idea was too narrow in focus and didn't consider the varied abilities of the people working in the organization. It is important to remember that any initiative must take into consideration that not everyone is on the same level as it relates to informational capacity and skills. All ideas should allow for differentiation so that everyone can apply them. Just as teachers should account for the various ability levels and learning styles of their students when designing a lesson, so should leaders who are generating ideas to be used by the diverse members of an organization. Remember that you must know the people you are working with, understand what they value, and consider their areas and levels of expertise. The end goal always is to create tools that serve the staff in serving the students in their learning.

Rejection helps to increase knowledge. With rejection comes the need to find answers. You will take the time to learn about the latest research and development regarding issues in your field that are relevant to your organization. The knowledge you have been relying on may not be enough to create the robust and comprehensive plan needed. And that's okay. The caveat is to now be willing to accept the deficit in knowledge as a potential area of professional improvement for yourself and to seek expert assistance in understanding that area. No one knows everything, so relax and open yourself to learning.

Finally, rejection makes you stronger. Working with others to design a better solution develops perseverance, stamina, and patience. The journey may be long and difficult. Through this process, you may struggle to remain consistent and focused. It will bring up deep from your memory your original purpose for venturing into this field. You will be reminded why you decided to become an educational leader and what your true purpose is in this role.

Consider when rejection occurs that forcing the wrong fit is often the culprit. Too often, new leaders enter an environment with a preconceived notion of how the organization should look. Their idea is based on previous experience or on places they feel are doing well and can serve as models to emulate. The greatest challenge with school reformation is the push to make one size fit all. It is common practice to use cookie cutter models in situations that are similar, believing such actions will yield similar results. But each organization is different. The same processes and methods cannot be used in different contexts. It is the leader's responsibility to take the time to analyze the context and identify the areas of improvement and the areas of strength. Yes, some ideas from other schools may be incorporated, but it should reasonably be expected that doing so may not duplicate the same positive results.

Another major cause for rejection is timing. Sufficient time must be allowed for collaboration in deciding how to prioritize, plan, and implement change. Community building results in trust in you as a leader and trust among the staff, but it will require continued positive interactions over time. The change you, as a leader, see as necessary may not be what members of the organization are capable of accomplishing at that time. The change you seek may not be yours to facilitate—it may be for the next leader to take on. To determine this, you must be tuned in to the climate of your new environment. Although there is always room for improvement in any school, be mindful that you are not meant to facilitate change in every area—you are there for a season.

## Thoughts on Rejection

- Leaders know how to manage rejection.
- Reflect on how ideas were developed, presented, and implemented. Was this process inclusive or done in isolation?
- You are the leader, but you are not the expert in all things.
- Use all critical feedback as a metric about the idea or the process. Not all complaints are full of hot air and noise.
- Your response to criticisms through your facial expressions, body language, and tone of voice indicate your thoughts and feelings. Always be aware.
- Use rejection to inspire your own growth and development.

> "A good leader is a person who takes a little more than his share of the blame and a little less than his share of the credit."
>
> – John Maxwell

# Know How to Practice Humility

# Servant Leadership Characteristics: Persuasion, Building Community

A s Principal Raymond looks around the large, open field behind the school, full of parents, students, and community members playing on carnival rides and eating treats, he has to smile. This is their second annual community fair, when the school celebrates the year's successes with the families and the community. Throughout this past year, Principal Raymond has often been asked how he led his building to become one of the top schools in the district in such a short time. These inquiries have been posed by the central office, sometimes media, and even some local legislators. He has been featured in several news articles and has been through a round of interviews on local television stations.

With all the attention focused on the successes of the school, and Principal Raymond being congratulated repeatedly for his work, one would think that he is pleased with the newfound fame. Quite the contrary, he is not enjoying the attention at all. However, he does use each opportunity to tell the story of the school and to acknowledge that the work was not achieved by his hands alone but also by the hands of the many parents and staff working together at the school. He is not comfortable taking credit for something he knows he could not have done alone. He understands that he is just one man with ideas. The real work had required many.

*So, today he celebrates with those who indeed are responsible for their shared ongoing success—with all the members of the school and the community family.*

When success is evident, longstanding, and exceeds the expectations of the public, the leaders of an organization can become haughty. When others constantly ask how you got to this point and people solicit your insight, it can be an intoxicating feeling. You may begin to feel self-assured, thinking that you have the stuff to get any job done. After all, the place was a mess when you took over—now look at it. Everyone who enters your building comments on how wonderful the place looks and how warm and inviting it feels. Hey, you did that. You turned this ship around, and you are sailing smoothly off into the sunset. It is easy to pat yourself on the back for being the sole catalyst for success, as if somehow you accomplished these successes on your own.

But quite frankly, as mentioned previously, it is impossible for one person to carry out all the work necessary to change the direction of an organization. Yes, one person may have conceptualized an idea, and one person could even have coordinated the series of events that set collective efforts in motion, but the work was implemented by many. So why do we sometimes think we are the only change agent? We are so confident that we challenge anyone who dares to contradict us because we know we can prove it—just look around!

Leaders often minimize the value of the work of the school community itself. It is easy to forget when you are the face of the organization as you begin to internalize the accolades. Beware that forgetting those who walked with you along the journey of highs and lows can be detrimental to the continued growth of the organization. How often have we been a part of an organization or a group and was rarely told "thank you"? How often have we simply wanted someone to tell us we were doing a good job? Can you recall how not being acknowledged made you feel?

Every person is important. There is no such thing as a worthless individual. Everyone is capable of adding to an effort in the name of furthering a vision, and people must feel appreciated for these efforts, particularly of their successes. Leaders must take the time to celebrate their people. Let the staff know you believe in the value of every person through your words and actions. Take the time to drop a note, say a kind word, give a certificate of recognition, or send an email message—there are so many ways to say thank you. Those small but genuine gestures help keep people motivated to continue working towards a common goal.

The people that make up your organization pay attention to your behavior toward not only themselves on the inside but also toward others. They note how you respond when people from outside of the organization give you praise. They listen for what you say and whether you give credit where credit is due. The slightest misstep of failing to acknowledge everyone's role in the successes can drop your leadership standing in their eyes. This misstep may not be intended, but the results can be harmful to the entire organization. Failing to express clearly that many individuals achieved the successes together, particularly to those outside of the organization who do not know of the inner workings and labors, will raise eyebrows. Those who are in the trenches will feel slighted. When you receive recognition from the public, be quick to emphasize that the efforts made were not yours alone.

The word *humility* has gotten a bad reputation, particularly in current society. Only the most brazen, boisterous, and domineering personalities are held in reverence as strong leaders. You can't be a good leader unless you are rude and overly confident, right? That idea seems to be the perspective that media portrays and society accepts as truth.

Humility is not often named as a characteristic people feel will take you to the top of your industry. However, being humble is not a sign of weakness. On the contrary, it resonates strength and courage. Humility is strength because you must stand against the temptations to accept selfish desires. This means you shy away for being full of self or braggadocio. You don't seek to do things with the intent of making a name for yourself or stimulating your own career path. You are comfortable with credit being given to the ones who deserve it. Humility displays courage. A humble leader is not afraid that allowing others to be recognized may damage his or her own career.

Being humble lets your people know that you need them as much as they need you. You help to steer, motivate, and keep the goal in focus in the minds of all. You accept your role as the face of the organization, but you do not allow that role to keep you from understanding your purpose and the value of others. You know that each person contributes and helps to provide all the necessary components to keep the organization growing and achieving. Humility may not be appreciated in today's society, but the confidence in your values and abilities and the purpose of your role in the organization far outweighs public perception of your leadership. And contrary to popular belief, the impact of your work will be just as relevant and memorable.

## Principle 5:  Know How to Practice Humility
### ❖ A Practical Exercise ❖

As you continue to grow in your position and school successes begin to add up, these suggestions will help keep you grounded and nurturing of the collaborative spirit of the staff.

1. Create a system to recognize individuals on staff frequently (e.g. Award Teacher-of-the-Week certificates).
2. Make public announcements acknowledging staff accomplishments, even those outside of school, so that students will be able to acknowledge their teachers as well.

3. Give personal thank you notes to staff, highlighting specific and positive things.
4. Encourage staff, individually and collectively, to initiate special projects using their talents and skills.
5. Send information to outside sources, such as news outlets, central office, and community organizations, about the great work the staff is doing.
6. Always say "Thank you!"

Being humble can be a very difficult characteristic to exhibit. As leaders, we are the ones that provide insight, direction, and support to those we lead. Demonstrating humbleness, admitting to not having the answers to everything, causes us to feel vulnerable and sometimes inadequate. We were chosen to lead because we had the skills and the competency needed to be successful. It seems contradictory to show any signs of weakness. With humility, what we would consider to be a weakness is a strength. The staff will support you knowing that you trust them to bring their expertise to the table on issues unfamiliar to you. This shared responsibility will create a bond that forms a foundation for continued collaboration and shared decision-making.

## Thoughts on Humility

- Leaders practice humility.

- One person cannot do the work. Acknowledge the reality that leadership understands how to coordinate the talents of many towards one goal.
- Honor the expertise of the people who work behind the scenes to get the work done.
- The fact that you may not know all things is not a sign of weakness but an opportunity for growth.
- Everyone wants to be thanked for a job done well.

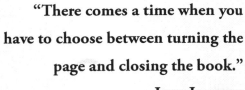

"There comes a time when you have to choose between turning the page and closing the book."

- JOSH JAMESON

Know When to Leave

# Servant Leadership Characteristics: Awareness, Foresight

M r. Phillips had been in his position as assistant principal for over ten years. He was well respected and had established a reputation for himself within the community as the enforcer of all things related to school policies and procedures. The new principal of the school had appreciated having a strong ally like Mr. Phillips on her team. She expected that he would help to keep the peace as she began to focus on revamping instructional matters. However, after a few months, Mr. Phillips was becoming more of a burden than a support.

Her vision included having all members of the leadership team participate in ongoing classroom walk-throughs and professional learning community meetings with staff, but Mr. Phillips had made it clear that he did not want to engage in such activities, and his focus had remained on discipline and procedures. As she agreed with Mr. Phillips that those things were indeed important, she also emphasized how it was as important, even more so, to make instructional issues a priority. Mr. Phillips had not seemed enthused or even interested, yet he grudgingly began to participate, mostly because he was all for compliance. As time went on, she realized that Mr. Phillips was not making any progress with handling this new set of responsibilities. In the classroom observations and PLC conversations, he still focused only on the disciplinary and procedural items—no instructional ones.

By the end of the year and after many conversations, off-site professional development, and personal support with instruction, she realized

*Mr. Phillips was not the right fit for the goals she was working toward. Although his strong stance on discipline and procedures had been needed when he first assumed the position, the culture had shifted and the climate of the building had become more subdued, allowing for instruction to now be the primary focus. Mr. Phillips could not accept that reality, and he showed an obvious reluctance to shift priorities. Whatever the reasons for his refusal to adapt, she knew that Mr. Phillips was no longer a good fit for the school.*

Have you ever heard the saying, "You have overstayed your welcomed"?

That statement is a reality for school leaders. Some remain at their post for several years. Complacency with the state of the school and the successes they have helped achieve creeps into the picture. It sometimes happens unexpectedly. You grind hard for many months, sometimes years, to get to a place of normalcy. People can now see those hard-fought changes you strived to make, so slow to manifest, from the outside. In the beginning, you had worked fifty-hour weeks, including weekends, and now you can actually go home at a decent hour. Those individuals you had dragged along kicking and screaming at the onset of the organizational change are now your biggest advocates and cheerleaders, especially to people entering the organization. You have finally arrived, and you want to enjoy the fruits of your labor. And although you intend to coast for a while, to regain your bearings, a sense of security slowly sets in. Before you know it, this is what you do, and it is working just fine. In your complacency, you have become a part of a new system where change is, again, not openly welcomed.

In some cases, success can lead to a false sense of security for the leaders and staff. Depending on how quickly the successes have come, the feeling of accomplishment and even invincibility can surface. People will be proud of what they have done and feel good about the progress. Celebration is deserved. But remember there is always room for improvement. Sometimes in our race to accomplish the goals we set, we feel that the work is done as soon as those goals are met. What else is there to do?

The constant evolution of standards, constituents, and society requires the organization to evolve as well. The need for new adjustments may not be immediately recognized as it may have gradually manifested, but it must be addressed. Those adjustments may impact some of the very foundational pillars erected to elicit the current success of the organization. The prospect of modifying the core of what the current success was built upon frightens people. "Why would we change the foundation of what brought us to this point? That's organizational suicide." Leaders and the staff sometimes have the mindset that whatever measures have brought success in the past should not be touched. It needs to be understood, however, that those pillars may have been suitable for past circumstances but are not necessarily suitable for present circumstances. It is perfectly fine to modify the foundation to help the organization grow.

Modifying the foundational pillars includes not only systems and procedures. It includes human capital as well, including the present leader. It is not easy to accept the fact that your season with the organization has come to an end. Because you were key in reaching this current state you may feel that it is your right to remain. It can be devastating to realize that it is not your destiny.

Let's look at this example to help with the understanding. When you first decide to become physically fit, you analyze your current state, seek out professional assistance at a local gym, and create a fitness program. You do a series of activities and exercises for a certain length of time. Over some months, you see some results. You like what you see, so you continue with the program. Eventually, you reach a plateau. You have lost the weight you set out to lose, and you have become stronger and more fit, but progress has stopped. You are still doing the same exercises that got you the results you are currently enjoying, so what is the problem? The fitness program was effective for the past physique you started with. As you became stronger and fitter, the exercises became less effective because they were used to correct the original problem areas. Now that those problem areas have been addressed, it is time to seek a new fitness program to address a new set of problem areas. There is nothing wrong with the exercises or your body. It is simply time to change the program to meet a new need.

The same is the case for leaders in an organization. You must realize that your time is limited. Your leadership style and skill set is meant for a particular time in an organization to address specific areas. But once those needs are met, two things can occur. You adjust your leadership style, committing to learn additional skills to enhance your role. Or you move to the next assignment. The first option is fine, if the modifications you make in yourself do not conflict with your value system. Do not modify your leadership style if it means compromising your moral being. You will risk operating in an arena that is not a true portrayal of who you are and what your purpose is. Remaining in a position at the risk of losing your true self is not worth the compromise.

It takes a confident individual to realize that you were placed in an organization because your specific skill set was needed at a specific time, not because you were needed forever. It is safe to say that most of us didn't believe we would stay in our first job until retirement. However, we should anticipate staying in a position for at least six months to a year. But what is the amount of time you need to change the course of an organization? No one has a specific length of time for how long change will take, so a leader needs to be prepared to move when the work is done.

You should not go into a situation thinking you will be at a certain organization for a predetermined amount of time. The danger of this mindset is that you will not perform at your maximum level; you must operate with dedication for the duration, regardless of when you might leave. You cannot shortchange the mission of the organization nor the people you have been charged to lead and serve in anticipation of the potential exit date. You are to be committed, every day, all day. Nevertheless, grounded and self-aware leaders understand that they can move an organization only so far, and they must allow others to move it further.

So, when is it time to make your exit? Will you see the signs? In other words, will you see changes in your attitude towards your contributions to the organization? Will you see changes in how people are responding to you and your ideas? More, will you heed them? It is important to be in tune with how things are developing within your organization and to be honest with yourself when assessing whether you are equipped to address those developments. Self-reflection is critical for an effective, thoughtful leader. The practice should be embedded in the thought process daily. Your thoughts and behavior should always be alignment with your moral being, your actions checked against your value system.

Furthermore, be mindful that your attitude may have shifted over time because of your achievements. Is your attitude one of humility? Or is it one of haughtiness and superiority? If educators in other positions of authority offer you suggestions that are met with contempt or a condescending manner, it may be time to leave. You see, you have reached the point where you believe you are "the expert" in this organization. There is little that anyone else can tell you, and you have become selective in who you are willing to learn from. That is a dangerous recipe for complacency, contempt, and resistance. And no leader should bear these characteristics.

## Principle 6: Know When to Leave
### ❖ A Practical Exercise ❖

If you are trying to determine if you should be thinking about moving on to another position, this exercise may be helpful in gauging your level of complacency. Use a journal or notebook to complete the steps below.

1. List the number of professional development events you have attended within the past six months.
2. List the number of scholarly research articles you have read within the past six months.
3. Based on the learning opportunities you have engaged in, how have you implemented the information in current practices, programs, or procedures? Have you created initiatives inspired by newly acquired professional development information?
4. How do you respond when you receive critical feedback about your leadership of the school?
5. What do you envision next steps for your current school to be? What possible projects are you excited about exploring?

If there has been little change in current practices despite your attending several trainings, or if you are extremely defensive about critical feedback, or if you have little interest in planning next steps for your school, you may be complacent in your role.

In my own career, I have been at that crossroad between deciding to remain or to move to the next opportunity. Although the work that I had accomplished was admirable and had created a culture of respect and growth for students and staff, the support I needed to continue this venture was not easily accessible or perhaps even available. This made the goals I wanted to accomplish even more difficult to reach. My passion to empower the students and staff in that school never waned, but I understood that maybe it was not meant for me to take the school to another level.

The timing of my decision to leave was strategically planned. Individuals in leadership were confident in their abilities to consistently carry forth the work and processes implemented to ensure continued daily operations. Leading up to my departure, there was ongoing conversation with staff about how working toward the goal was imperative, regardless of the leadership. It was not easy to have that conversation with staff about my transition to the next venture. The decision caused much sadness and shock as I shared it with others, but I made sure to let them know that I believed the work accomplished up to that point was a result of teamwork. I stressed that they were more than capable of moving forward without me and that the students still needed a one hundred percent daily effort from them. With my helping to transition the new leadership into my former role and providing ongoing encouragement to staff, the change became more bearable.

This chapter is not meant to tell you when or even how to leave, but the principle is important to include in terms of laying out your career in leadership. With each position you enter, your time to leave will come. The question is whether you leave voluntarily or you allow the circumstances in your organization to force you out. Although being compelled to leave is not uncommon, it is much better to leave on your own terms. Write your own narrative; don't let it be written for you.

## Thoughts on Leaving

- Leaders know when to leave.
- Reflect on and analyze your attitude towards your current situation. Do you feel you are growing? Or do you feel you are in a rut?
- Are you becoming increasingly despondent and negative towards organizational compliance, rules, and procedures? This may be a sign that your values are no longer aligned to the organization or that you are unwilling or unable to adjust to the new direction of the organization.
- Leaving is not quitting. It is acknowledging that it is time for others to grow in leadership.

- Leaving with a smooth transition plan does not disrupt school operations or culture.
- Leaving in a timely manner retains your integrity and keeps your reputation respectable.

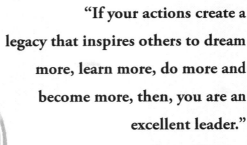

"If your actions create a
legacy that inspires others to dream
more, learn more, do more and
become more, then, you are an
excellent leader."

— DOLLY PARTON

Know Your Impact

## Servant Leadership Characteristics: Commitment to Growth, Conceptualization

*A*mber is exhausted and just wants to go home, put up her tired feet, and eat dinner from her favorite Mexican restaurant. It is a carry-out order, and she hopes her wait won't be long. Standing in line, she hears her name being called from behind. When she turns, she sees a table of five, all former teachers of hers, eating dinner. After she picks up her food, she walks over to speak to them. It has been over four years since they worked together. Looking at their open and smiling faces, she remembers how it had been a struggle for most of them adjusting to the changing culture of the school and community.

*They begin to share with her their current positions: two are instructional coaches, two are teacher leads in their building, and one is in a leadership program while serving as an assessment coordinator. They all seem to be doing well and mention that they try to meet once a month to stay in touch. They state how they had bonded when they were at her school because they relied on one another for support. Surprisingly, they thank her for her leadership, support, and constant motivation to use their talents to make things better for kids. They say that her ongoing belief in their abilities and her insight had given them the confidence and courage to do the work and to apply for their current positions. One says that Amber was one of the best principals she ever had.*

*After exchanging contact information, they all decide that she would be invited to the next monthly dinner. Getting in her car, the exhaustion Amber felt entering the restaurant doesn't seem so heavy now. She hadn't realized how much she had impacted that staff, as challenging as those circumstances were. She never would have imagined. She's glad she decided to have Mexican tonight.*

Despite how you leave an assignment, believe that you have made an impact. Every word, action, and decision we make in life impacts those with whom we interact. Nothing we do or say is ever in isolation. We make an impact, be it negative or positive, wherever we go. Our impact may be immediately seen—someone says thank you when you open the door for them—or it may be something remembered by the recipient when we are no longer anywhere around. The depth and breadth of the effects may not be realized for months or even years.

Gratitude and acknowledgement can be very hard to come by, regardless of who it is you work with. During your time of service, you may often wonder if you are making a difference. But know that you have influenced the lives of those with whom you have worked, the community that you served, the staff who supported your work, and the public's perception of your organization.

There are four areas of impact to consider: professional, personal, community, and universal. Professionally, as a leader you helped to build capacity in the people you were charged to lead. Through your leadership, exposure to research-based best practices was facilitated in the training you provided. You provided opportunities for collegial conversation and support that encouraged the professional growth of your people. You challenged their way of thinking, planning, and assessing themselves through their daily activities. You helped individuals to develop a set of skills that will continue to make them marketable, and you helped build a foundation for additional professional learning.

Personally, the impact is just as transformative. When you treat people with respect, value their expertise, and allow them to build their capacity, you have made a difference. People will remember how you allowed them to take risks and make mistakes without being fearful of retribution. They will remember how you encouraged them to be creative, listened to their ideas, and allowed them to implement the resulting projects. They will remember how you provided honest, timely feedback that helped them develop and grow stronger and more confident. They will also remember how you understood and empathized with them when they were facing personal challenges. They will appreciate your genuine care and transparency in word and action. The time a smile was given or a kind word shared could have been the time you reset someone's thoughts about giving up. Personal lives have been shifted, and people will now consider emulating your attitude, behaviors, and actions when they work with others in the future.

As a community, the work ethics, systems, and procedures created and implemented to build a community of collaboration and trust will remain within the organization. The embedded cultural values in which every stakeholder invested will continue to resonate long after you have gone. People who were a part of the process for developing these systems and procedures have a vested interested in overseeing their continued success. They will insist on pushing this important work forward and advocating for consistency in the use of the procedures and systems. As new individuals come on board, these valuable systems will be taught again. Eventually, this will be the way of life for the organization. It will be "just what we do here." Furthermore, there will always be the space for collaboration and learning that will allow for modifications to current processes, as needed. You engaged people with a process that clearly showed that you valued their voice and input. This will continue as a part of the cycle of learning throughout the organization.

Finally, there is the universal impact. Within a school setting, your interaction with students and their families, indirectly through the staff or directly, has great effect. Allowing families to engage in the process of their students' learning will transform their interpretations of schools and their purpose forever. When families and students are invited to participate and invest in the educational experience, these interactions lay a fresh foundation for how they continue on in education. The nurturing support and posed challenges the students experience will allow them to become self-motivated to strive for success because you and the staff took the time to develop their character and thinking. Families will continue to hold up their students through school and even through life after positive and encouraging interactions with you and your staff. These families are empowered; their opinions and thoughts were heard and validated, and now they will seek to build on their strengths and will desire to do more for themselves and their students. Their involvement and commitment will spread within that school community and beyond. The universal type of impact is like the rock thrown in the middle of the pond; the ripples will be seen and felt way far from the point of impact.

But just as your impact can be positive, it can be negative as well. When you accomplish work through means that do not value the people of the organization, misrepresent the people you are there to serve, or place your personal agenda ahead of that of the organization, you generate a negative residual in the four areas of impact.

It is likely though that you have done much more positive than negative, especially if your values and principles lead you on your journey. The exercise below is a powerful tool to help you record and reflect on your power as a leader and the legacy you will someday leave behind.

## Principle 7: Know Your Impact
### ❖ A Reflection Exercise ❖

Journaling is an excellent way to be mindful of what you are doing in your position. In a journal or notebook, list several stakeholder categories of the school or organization that you serve (i.e. parents, students, staff, community, outreach, etc.). Write every day, or at least weekly, about your attitude, behavior, decisions, and actions that have impacted the stakeholders listed. After several weeks, you will have a powerful account of what you have done and how you have positively or negatively affected your school and the greater community. Let reading back over your writing be a constant challenge for you to ever improve your leadership abilities as the details help you stay self-aware, humble, and focused. Also important, your journaling will serve as a powerful medium for you to share your story with others.

It is very difficult to understand the impact you make upon the people you serve and lead. During my years of working in various environments, I often questioned my skills and my decision to become a leader. But there are also many bright spots that immediately reveal themselves to me, that illuminate how I helped a student understand a concept as a teacher, or helped a teacher strengthen her understanding of an instructional strategy. There are occasional *thank you*'s and small tokens of appreciation. Really, it wasn't until years later, when I would run into former students and staff, that they let me know just how important I was in influencing them to develop into the people they were. Those conversations remind me just how impactful this work is, even if I don't receive recognition or see immediate results. Those individuals have shown me that impact can change lives.

The most important question you will answer in this entire book is, What legacy do you want to create for yourself? This question should be one of the first you tackle when you move into a new organization. It will be one of the guiding principles you will use as you work to build the organization, develop the people you lead, and support the ones you serve.

Lasting, lifelong impact you will make. There is no question about that. It is up to you to decide what kind of impact it will be.

## Thoughts on Impact

- Leaders know their impact.
- List each area, project, or idea developed and implemented when you were leading. Who was involved? What was the outcome?
- If the decisions you made were not contradictory to your moral foundation and were best for your children, you made a positive impact.
- Impact may not be immediate, but remember that someone's life was touched by your words and actions.
- You will have no regrets if you were sincere in your leadership.
- Negative legacies are hard to forget. Positive legacies are hard to change.

"The scariest moment is always just
before you start."

— STEPHEN KING

Final Thoughts

## We Wear the Mask
## Paul Laurence Dunbar, 1872 – 1906

We wear the mask that grins and lies,
It hides our cheeks and shades our eyes,—
This debt we pay to human guile;
With torn and bleeding hearts we smile,
And mouth with myriad subtleties.

Why should the world be over-wise,
In counting all our tears and sighs?
Nay, let them only see us, while
    We wear the mask.

We smile, but, O great Christ, our cries
To thee from tortured souls arise.
We sing, but oh the clay is vile
Beneath our feet, and long the mile;
But let the world dream otherwise,
We wear the mask!

Paul Laurence Dunbar wrote "We Wear the Mask" [1] in 19th-century America. The poem poignantly portrays how Black people hid their pain and frustration about their current situation from Whites and even from one other. To be transparent and honest about how they felt during this time would likely result in persecution, even death. Oppression and blatant discrimination was a way of life, and it was clear, at least then, that there was no recourse because Blacks had no voice in the justice system. Further, they would hide their true feelings from one another to avoid compounding the defeat, desperation, and anxiety already prevalent throughout the Black community. So, many wore "the mask" that displayed contentment and hid the pain with varying degrees of success.

This poem holds a sad truth about the current state of our educational systems and the leaders within. There are many people walking around wearing masks. They do not want to openly acknowledge that the current reforms being applied to many of our priority districts and schools are barely addressing the dishearteningly deep issues and challenges. They are aware that more needs to be done or be done more differently, but they either choose to appear content or they show their frustration in not knowing how to push back.

We have failed our children and their families by not seeking out and facing the truth. The truth is, people are the X factor to substantially transform our school systems. The truth has merely been skimmed, if not completely overlooked by many. Could it be because the solution is so simple? To invest in the people? Developing and supporting our school leaders should be the highest priority of the masses, from government officials to business people, from educators to everyday citizens.

No drive-by professional development sessions or two-day institutes will begin to fundamentally address the need for knowledgeable, competent, and confident educational leaders. All initial teacher preparation and ongoing training and education must be purposeful and intentional.

Schools and educational systems have never been one-dimensional. They are multi-faceted with ever-moving parts, fragile and susceptible to constant internal and external influences: new policies, new superintendent visions, new strategic plans, and new standards. The only stable factors in educational organizations are the leaders and staff that make up the schools, the all-important professionals. So why not hone in on investing in our leaders who potentially hold the widest berth of influence?

Creating effective leaders is a huge undertaking. It cannot be accomplished by emulating a specific model or program. True leadership development first starts with examining the leaders themselves. Twenty years of educational experience leads me to conclude that there exist some foundational principles to follow that help form strong leaders. Although those principles are general knowledge in the sense that people may have heard of them before, these seven principles have not been exercised collectively to yield the influence necessary to make a significant difference in the education of our children.

As with any shift in thinking and behavior, time is a factor to consider. No one remedy can be an overnight fix for a situation that has been decades in the making. But helping leaders—and those who hold leaders accountable—to understand the great amount of time and effort necessary to improve upon the current state of many public schools is paramount. As in Dunbar's poem, too many school leaders are wearing masks. We are afraid to speak up and seek guidance with leading schools for fear we will be criticized, ostracized, or eliminated from the position. Even amongst colleagues in our professional networks, the specific challenges and frustrations of the job are not often discussed for fear of judgment and confirmation of perceived hopelessness in meeting the demands of the position.

Still, the conversation must begin sooner rather than later. We need to remove the masks. We need to expose the painful yet truthful concerns of being educational leaders in challenging environments. Once we acknowledge the reality—not the often-skewed perception of truth—only then can we begin to truly transform education.

References

## REFERENCES

### Truth Provides Understanding and Transforms Educational Leaders

1. Truth. (accessed July 8, 2016). In *Dictionary.com*. Retrieved from http:// www.dictionary.com/truth

2. Understanding. (accessed July 18, 2016). In *Dictionary.com*. Retrieved from http://www.dictionary.com/understanding

3. Lindsey, R. B., Robins, K. N., & Terrell, R. D. (2009). *Cultural proficiency: A manual for school leaders.* Thousand Oaks, CA: Corwin Press.

4. Bulkley, K. E., & Burch, P. (2011). The changing nature of private engagement in public education: For-profit and nonprofit organizations and educational reform. *Peabody Journal of Education, 86*(3), 236–251.

5. Gregory, A., Skiba, R. J., & Noguera, P. A. (2010). The achievement gap and the discipline gap: Two sides of the same coin? *Educational Researcher, 39*(1), 59–68.

Skiba, R. J., Horner, R. H., Chung, C. G., Rausch, M. K., May, S. L., & Tobin, T. (2011). Race is not neutral: A national investigation of African American and Latino disproportionality in school discipline. *School Psychology Review*, *40*(1), 85.

6. Camera, L. (2015, December 15). High school graduation rates hit record high. *US News.* Retrieved from http://www.usnews.com/news/articles/2015-12-15/high-school-graduation-rates-hit-record-high

7. Tomlinson, C. A. (2001). *How to differentiate instruction in mixed-ability classrooms*. Retrieved from http://www.ascd.org/publications/books/101043.aspx

## Creating Great Schools

1. Eberly Center for Teaching Excellence and Educational Innovation. (n.d.). *Whys and hows of assessment*. Retrieved from University of Carnegie Mellon University website: https:// www.cmu.edu/teaching/assessment/ basics/formative-summative.html

2. Eberly Center for Teaching Excellence and Educational Innovation. (n.d.). *Whys and hows of assessment*. Retrieved from University of Carnegie Mellon University website: https://www.cmu.edu/teaching/assessment/ basics/formative-summative.html

3. Maxwell, T. W., & Thomas, A. R. (1991). School climate and school culture. *Journal of Educational Administration, 29*(2), 72–82.

   Brucato, J. M. (2005). Creating a learning environment: An educational leader's guide to managing school culture. Lanham, MD: Scarecrow Press.

4. Barth, R. S. (2006). Improving relationships within the schoolhouse. *Educational Leadership, 63*(6), 8.

5. Autry, J. A. (2001). *The servant leader: How to build a creative team, develop great morale, and improve bottom-line performance.* New York, NY: Random House.

## Servant Leadership and Your Assignment

1. Spears, L. C. (1996). Reflections on Robert K. Greenleaf and servant leadership. *Leadership and Organization Development Journal, 17*(7), 33–35.

2. Spears, L. C. (1996). Reflections on Robert K. Greenleaf and servant leadership. *Leadership and Organization Development Journal, 17*(7), 33–35.

3. Kiechel, W. (1998). The leader as servant. In L. C. Spears (Ed.), *Reflections on leadership: Service, stewardship, spirit, and*

*servant-leadership* (pp. 121–125). Hoboken, NJ: John Wiley and Sons.

4. Taylor, C. (2002). *Geography of the "new" education market.* Aldershot, UK: Ashgate.

5. Maxwell, J. C. (2005). *Developing the leader within you.* Nashville, TN: Thomas Nelson, Inc.

6. Abel, C. F. (2002). Academic success and the international student: Research and recommendations. *New Directions for Higher Education, (117),* 13–20.

7. Abel, C. F. (2002). Academic success and the international student: Research and recommendations. *New Directions for Higher Education, (117),* 13–20.

8. Abel, C. F. (2002). Academic success and the international student: Research and recommendations. *New Directions for Higher Education, (117),* 13–20.

9. Kouzes, J. M., & Posner, B. Z. (2011). *Credibility: How leaders gain and lose it, why people demand it.* Hoboken, NJ: John Wiley and Sons.

10. Abel, C. F. (2002). Academic success and the international student: Research and recommendations. *New Directions for Higher Education, (117)*, 13–20.

11. Taylor, C. (2002). *Geography of the "new" education market.* Aldershot, UK: Ashgate.

12. Taylor, C. (2002). *Geography of the "new" education market.* Aldershot, UK: Ashgate.

13. Spears, L. C. (1996). Reflections on Robert K. Greenleaf and servant leadership. *Leadership and Organization Development Journal, 17*(7), 33–35.

14. Foresight. (accessed July 20, 2016). In *Dictionary.com.* Retrieved from http:// www.dictionary.com/foresight Spears, L. C. (1996). Reflections on Robert K. Greenleaf and servant leadership. *Leadership and Organization Development Journal, 17*(7), 33–35.

15. Sendjaya, S., Sarros, J. C., & Santora, J. C. (2008). Defining and measuring servant leadership behaviour in organizations. *Journal of Management Studies, 45*(2), 402–424.

16. Abel, C. F. (2002). Academic success and the international student: Research and recommendations. *New Directions for Higher Education, (117)*, 13–20.

## Know Who You Are

1. Barth, R. S. (2006). Improving relationships within the schoolhouse. *Educational Leadership, 63*(6), 8.

2. Deal, T. E., & Peterson, K. D. (1990). The principal's role in shaping school culture. Washington, DC: Office of Educational Research and Improvement.

3. Craig, S. E. (2016). The Trauma-Sensitive Teacher. *Educational Leadership, 74*(1), 28–32.

## Know Who You Serve

1. National Assessment of Education Progress (NAEP). Retrieved from http://www.nces.ed.gov

2. Camera, L. (2015, December 15). High school graduation rates hit record high. *US News.* Retrieved from http://www.usnews.com/news/articles/2015-12-15/high-school-graduation-rates-hit-record-high

3. Argyris, C. (2006). *Overcoming organizational defenses: Facilitating organizational learning* (2nd ed.). Upper Saddle River, NJ: Prentice Hall.

4. Senge, P. M. (2006). *The fifth discipline: The art and practice of the learning organization.* New York, NY: Random House.

5. Brown, Y. F. (n.d.). *The ladder of inference: How assumptions can cause misconceptions. JAD Communications.* Retrieved from http://www.jadcommunications.com/ yvonnefbrown Argyris, C. (1990). *Overcoming organizational defenses: Facilitating organizational learning* (2nd ed.). Upper Saddle River, NJ: Prentice Hall.

6. Senge, P. M. (2006). *The fifth discipline: The art and practice of the learning organization.* New York, NY: Random House.

7. Cross, T. L., Bazron, B. J., Dennis, K. W., & Issacs, M. R. (1993*). Toward a culturally competent system of care: Vol 2.* Washington, DC: Georgetown University, Child Development Center, Child and Adolescent Service System Program, Technical Assistance Center.

8. Lindsey, R. B., Robins, K. N., & Terrell, R. D. (Eds.). (2009). *Cultural proficiency: A manual for school leaders* (3rd ed.). Thousand Oak, CA: Corwin Press.

9. Lindsey, R. B., Robins, K. N., & Terrell, R. D. (Eds.). (2009). *Cultural proficiency: A manual for school leaders* (3rd ed.). Thousand Oak, CA: Corwin Press.

10. Lindsey, R. B., Robins, K. N., & Terrell, R. D. (Eds.). (2009). *Cultural proficiency: A manual for school leaders* (3rd ed.). Thousand Oak, CA: Corwin Press.

## Final Thoughts

1. Dunbar, P. L. (1896). We wear the mask. *Lyrics of lowly life*. New York, NY: Dodd, Mead, and Co.

# About The Author

## About Antoinette Pearson, Ed.D

Antoinette Pearson, Ed.D. is the Founder, and Lead Consultant of Common Sense Learning, LLC. An educator of 20 years, Dr. Pearson has worked in various capacities in the public school system including: a teacher, curriculum leader, assistant principal, athletic director, principal, and now a consultant helping educators of various levels. Her determination and passion for creating equitable opportunities for children led to her advancement in the education field.

Known as education's change agent, Antoinette is passionate about equitable opportunities for learning. This passion for equity is evident from her participation in the following programs: Michigan Department of Education's African American Young Men of Promise Initiative, Harvard School of Education's School Transformation Leaders' Institute (2013) and Family Engagement Institute (2014).

Antoinette is also an educational author and speaker. She speaks and authors from the perspective of an experienced urban educator, change agent, and a nurturing mother. Her new book Truth Transforms Education is available now on her website; www.antoinettepearson.com.

Follow Antoinette on social media.

Facebook:      @DrAntoinettePearson

Twitter:       @Dr_APearson

Instagram:     DrAntoinettePearson

Made in the USA
Lexington, KY
21 January 2017